AUTHENTIC COMMUNITY

SIX PRACTICES OF CHRIST-CENTERED RELATIONSHIPS

JASON LOHSE

AUTHENTIC COMMUNITY
SIX PRACTICES OF CHRIST-CENTERED RELATIONSHIPS

Jason Lohse

ISBN: 9780982638293
Religion – Christian Life – Adult

Library of Congress Control Number: 2018930057

Italics and bold highlights in Scripture references are the author's emphasis.

All quotes offered in this book are for inspirational purposes only and are not intended in any way to be or imply an indorsement of the quoted author or their fully written works.

To order additional copies of this resource online, go to: http://jasonlohse.com.
For invoice billing requests on bulk orders, contact: info@jasonlohse.com.

Cover and interior design by Jason Lohse (openskypublishing.com)
Edited by Karen Steinmann (karstein@tx.rr.com)

Printed in the United States of America
Published by Open Sky Publishing
Website: http://openskypublishing.com

Special thanks to Steve Roach, Steve Smothers and Jenny Lohse for your encouragement and participation in the development of this resource.

Table of Contents

Welcome to Authentic Community!

The Holy Spirit has poured out Christ's new life into our hearts, creating a greater capacity for us to experience deeper relationships with our brothers and sisters in Christ. As we follow Jesus, the depth of love and connection we discover in relationship with Him will be unmistakably evident within our community.

"You were taught, with regard to your former way of life, to put off your old self, which is being corrupted by its deceitful desires; to be made new in the attitude of your minds; and to put on the new self, created to be like God in true righteousness and holiness."
– Ephesians 4:22-24

Introduction

In Ephesians 4:17-32, the Apostle Paul describes a believer's journey out of spiritual darkness into Christ-likeness—a life-changing path that radically transforms our thinking, attitudes, and behavior. In verse 25, notice Paul's natural progression and where he turns his focus: toward Christ-centered relationships.

"Love aligns our hearts to the lives we're supposed to live."
— Erwin Raphael McManus

It's in the context of Christ-centered relationships that our "new self" in Jesus Christ is nurtured, tested, and proven. In these verses, Paul encourages six practices that promote spiritual maturity and community among believers now poised within the Body of Christ to experience kingdom increase and missional impact.

A Better Position

As believers in Jesus Christ, we've not just been called *out* of something but called *into* something. God calls us out of the world's system of values and into something better—life in community with the family of God. When we begin to do life together with our spiritual family, we position ourselves for life as God intended. As you walk with other believers, united together in Christ, there is power, fullness, and purpose not typically found in a life of isolation.

"[1] How good and pleasant it is when God's people live together in unity!"
— Psalm 133:1

Part of our old way of life included living independently of others, but the way of Jesus is not meant to be lived alone. If we're going it alone, then we're not going in the way God intended. If God Himself exists in community (Father, Son, and Holy Spirit), then it's clear to see we need community even more. As we follow God's example of intimate connection, then we, too, find that being rightly and wholeheartedly connected with other Christ-followers offers the best environment for navigating our spiritual journey.

Each of us have been embedded with the Holy Spirit of God with the intent that the life we live will express the life of God in us.

A Deeper Gratification

In our culture today, technology is shaping how we interact and experience relationships. Though virtual community can add a level of feeling connected, it's not a viable substitute for the life-giving encounters—those real, personal, face-to-face interactions—that we need to experience true fulfilment in Christ. God has wired us to find satisfaction in deep, heart-level relationships—the kind of relationships we can only access in Christ-centered community.

For many followers of Jesus, real community is a familiar theory but a foreign experience. The truth is that most of us struggle with knowing how to be our authentic selves, even among friends. This desire for authentic relationships, where others know "the real me," is often hindered by common struggles we all share—negative experiences in the past as well as the fear of the unknown. A trusted approach like what we find in Ephesians 4:25-32 offers relational touch points with accessible and clear boundaries so everyone can find greater fulfilment in living unguarded from the inside out.

For many followers of Jesus, real community is a familiar theory but a foreign experience.

A Greater Identity

The process of becoming authentic involves not only our relationship with God and our community but how we relate with ourselves. The foundation of being able to love anyone else is learning how to love ourselves and gratefully embracing who God made us to be. Genuine spiritual connection with others rises out of understanding and accepting who we are in Christ Jesus.

*"[31] Love your neighbor **as you love yourself.**"*
— Mark 12:31

Authenticity is not about imitating someone else but about emerging fully alive within God's incredible design, embracing the person God originally imagined us to become and achieving our God-given potential. He has intentionally fashioned our distinct personality to accent certain aspects of His heart, His mind, and His ways. Authentic community creates an environment in which each person can discover and pursue his or her own unique contribution to God's kingdom.

*"[10] Therefore, as we have opportunity, let us do good to all people, **especially to those who belong to the family of believers.**"*
— Galatians 6:10

A Stronger Family

We will never recognize our spiritual destiny without first recognizing our spiritual family. Fulfilling our potential requires that we take our relationships with other Christ-followers seriously. God's purpose is to bring us into holy relationship with Himself and into whole relationship with others. These are not mutually exclusive but an integral part of His greater plan. We have the responsibility and the privilege to reflect God's character in the way we interact with our community. In this spiritual family, we find the encouragement to change and become like Christ in how we love, care, serve, encourage, challenge, confront, forgive, grow, work, and celebrate together.

"The more conscious I am of what God has yet to do in me, the less critical I am of what He has yet to do in others."
— Andy Stanley

The Holy Spirit, who has come to live in us, revolutionizes our ability to see every person as valuable to God and to envision how they can become fully alive in the Body of Christ. This shift from "me" to "we" is the process of bringing our vertical life with Christ into our horizontal life for healthy, life-giving connection with others. As we remove walls of separation, we will discover a God-infused strength to overcome obstacles, fight temptation, ignite passion, and clarify direction.

*"[23] And this is his command: to believe in the name of his Son, Jesus Christ, and to **love one another as he commanded us.**"*
— 1 John 3:23

A Wider Legacy

Through authentic community, our hearts and lives are shaped to influence the world around us. As followers of Christ, living a life of authenticity can change the world even after we've left it. Every one of us is challenged to leave a legacy of faithfulness. How we practice and express our new Christ-life can impact how others experience authentic community for years to come.

*"[14] May I never boast except in the cross of our Lord Jesus Christ, through which the world has been crucified to me, and I to the world. [15] Neither circumcision nor uncircumcision means anything; **what counts is the new creation.** [16] Peace and mercy to all who follow this rule . . ."*
— Galatians 6:14-16

God has given us the privilege and responsibility to influence others through our lives. These friends, family members, co-workers, and others surrounding us need to witness the way we love, the way we live, and the way we lead with genuine humility, real conviction, and true joy. When a person is willing to root out all selfishness, falsehood, and pride, the authenticity of God's life shines through, attracting others who long to experience and pursue life in Christ along with us.

Every person in the world is created in God's image, but the "new creations" in Christ are the ones who can truly demonstrate what God is like. May God give us the grace to open our lives and the courage to engage our hearts with the hope of sharing many incredible "God experiences" together, as we live out our call of authentic community in Jesus Christ.

How To Use This Book

Authentic Community was written to guide you and your community on your journey toward putting on the "new self" in Christ. This resource is designed to encourage your spiritual maturity and help you growth in authenticity together as you engage and build upon the 6 "practices" of Christ-centered relationships:

1. **SPEAK UP** WITH HONESTY. [Acceptance] leads to security.
2. **MAKE UP** QUICKLY WITH OTHERS. [Restoration] leads to healing.
3. **STEP UP** AND DO MY PART. [Trust] leads to intimacy.
4. **BUILD UP** WITH MY WORDS. [Encouragement] leads to confidence.
5. **KEEP UP** WITH THE SPIRIT'S LEADING. [Accountability] leads to growth.
6. **GIVE UP** MY GRUDGES. [Forgiveness] leads to freedom.

"[2] My goal is that they may be encouraged in heart and united in love, so that they may have the full riches of complete understanding, in order that they may know the mystery of God, namely, Christ..."
— Colossians 2:2

With this in mind, *Authentic Community* will lead you through a 7-session study focused on Ephesians 4:25-32. There is 1 "Welcome" session for your initial group gathering and 6 main sessions around each "practice." Each practice includes a weekly session containing:

- An **INTRODUCTION** at the beginning of each session with insights and direction to help set the tone around the weeks "practice."

- **5 DAILY READINGS** that includes Scripture and questions for individual study and reflection prior to the next group meeting time.

- A **GROUP TIME: NOTES** page to jot down thoughts, ideas, and experiences to highlight and share in your Group Meeting time.

- **GROUP MEETINGS** that encourage sharing and reflecting on the daily readings, with questions for deeper discussion and application.

- The **LEADERS GUIDE** provides "ice breakers," ministry insights, teaching ideas, and helpful tips to assist anyone leading the group.

- The **MY RESPONSE** page is for writing down prayer needs and identifying next steps. Each group meeting with conclude with a time of prayer and ministry for needs within the group.

"[16] All Scripture is God-breathed and is useful for teaching, rebuking, correcting and training in righteousness, [17] so that the servant of God may be thoroughly equipped for every good work."
— 2 Timothy 3:16-17

Genuine, faithful participation by each person in these activities will strengthen the groups ability to experience authentic community.

Group Time: Notes

As you study and read through *Authentic Community*, feel free to underline statements, highlight ideas, and write down your thoughts in the margin. Use this "Group Time: Notes" section to record inspirational quotes and what God reveals to you through Scripture and conversation with your community.

Pursuing personal authenticity is an expression of love for God and who He's made us to be, allowing us the incredible privilege of being a blessing to others.

"I continue to dream and pray about a revival of holiness in our day that moves forth in mission and creates authentic community."
— John Wesley

Group Time - Session 1

Let's Start Talking

Anyone ever involved in a small group has an idea of what the perfect community experience would be like. With each new opportunity comes fresh aspirations for the future, but for some of us, the idea of community resurrects nightmares from the past. Perhaps it conjures up the anxiety you felt years ago when attending a first group meeting, like the inner turmoil of an awkward blind date that you knew didn't stand a chance the moment you walked in the door. Or maybe it transports you back in time to a meeting in which you felt like you were attending someone else's family reunion—where everybody knew all the inside jokes except for you.

A follower of Jesus who is maturing will love differently, think differently, act differently and build relationships differently than he or she did before they came to faith in Christ.

Yet despite a few bad experiences, let's start fresh, entering this new group study with a new attitude, just as Ephesians 4:22-24 encourages us to do. Let's see this small group study as a new opportunity to create the best community we've ever hoped to experience. No group is perfect, but focusing on the positive proves a perfect place to begin. Remember: community is about discovering "common unity." It's the perfect time to be reminded that we have more in common than we may realize.

1. What motivated you to participate in this group? Who invited you?

*"[16] **So from now on we regard no one from a worldly point of view.** Though we once regarded Christ in this way, we do so no longer. [17] Therefore, if anyone is in Christ, the new creation has come: The old has gone, the new is here!"*
— 2 Corinthians 5:16-17

2. What are you most hopeful to gain as a result of being in the group and going through this *Authentic Community* study?

3. What is the one word that would best describe the season of life you're in right now? Share a little about why you choose that word.

Group Time - Session 1

Week In Review

Take a few minutes to look back through the introduction to this session. Share with your group any points that stood out to you and what ideas pique your interest to learn more about in this study.

"Don't judge a man by where he is, because you don't know how far he has come."
— C. S. Lewis

Let's Bring It Home

If there were one word to sum up the heart's desire of every Christ-follower, it would be the word "*authentic*." The word "authentic" comes from the root word "author" and is related to the word "authority"; being "authentic" means you have authority or proof through undeniable evidence that a person is who he or she claims to be.

All persons are valued by the community for who they are in Christ, not just where they are in process.

Authenticity simply means, "I know you."

People ascribe authenticity to us when our *outside* world matches our *inside* world. By the grace of Jesus, Christ-followers have become a new creation on the inside. He has made us righteous and holy through His redemptive work on the cross. From God's perspective, this is who we REALLY are. The old self we used to be is now dead. The new self is fully alive, and we have the freedom and permission to live from it.

*"[30] It is because of him that you are in Christ Jesus, who has become for us wisdom from God—**that is, our righteousness, holiness and redemption.**"*
— 1 Corinthians 1:30

Authentic community seeks to empower every person to express outwardly the real person he or she is inwardly. Our sin and brokenness has greatly distorted how we perceive ourselves, God, and others, but God desires to restore our ability to engage the abundant life Jesus paid for with His own life. Understanding the reality of our God-given identity helps us love others as they are, for who they are, wherever they are on their journey with Christ and within our community.

*"[28] He is the one we proclaim, admonishing and teaching everyone with all wisdom, so that **we may present everyone fully mature in Christ.**"*
— Colossians 1:28

1. Read Ephesians 4:22-24 (page 8). What does it mean to "put on the new self" if you've already been made a new creation in Christ?

Group Time - Session 1

"[16] ***So from now on we regard no one from a worldly point of view.*** *Though we once regarded Christ in this way, we do so no longer.* [17] *Therefore, if anyone is in Christ, the new creation has come: The old has gone, the new is here!"*
— 2 Corinthians 5:16-17

2. Why does Scripture require us "to be made new in our mind" and begin thinking about ourselves like God does? Why is it so easy to tolerate and overlook this kind of unbelief in our true identity?

4. What one-word attributes come to mind when you think about your "authentic self," the "new self" you are in Christ? Share these words out loud as a group, as many as come to heart and mind.

If there were one word to sum up the essence of God's desire for every Christ-follower, it would be the word "*community*." God Himself embodies this example of community in the Trinity (Father, Son, and Holy Spirit) and models an intimate relationship that is mutually beneficial. Each Person of the Godhead glories in and will eternally enjoy the exaltation of the other. What a powerful picture of authentic community and a worthy example for us to pursue with one another!

"[14] *May the grace of the Lord Jesus Christ, and the love of God, and the fellowship of the Holy Spirit be with you all."*
— 2 Corinthians 13:14

In order to experience deeper, healthier relationships, we should reconsider how Scripture describes healthy interaction within the Body of Christ. While no quality relationship is without its risks and some emotional pain is inevitable along the way, the level of authenticity we strive for will influence the course of our lives and the lives of those whom we touch.

1. What do you find inspiring about God's example of community?

2. What risks are involved in building deeper relationships? What are the potential outcomes, both positive and negative?

3. Which truth, insight or idea from this session encourages you the most?

My Response - Session 1

My Prayer Needs:

My Groups Prayer Needs:

My Next Step:

"[20] My prayer is not for them alone. I pray also for those who will believe in me through their message, [21] ***that all of them may be one, Father, just as you are in me and I am in you.*** *May they also be in us* **so that the world may believe that you have sent me.** *[22] I have given them the glory that you gave me,* ***that they may be one as we are one...***"
—John 17:20-22

Speak Up with Honesty.

How do we get to the place in our relationships where we are real and not fake, where we are honest and genuine with one another?

[Acceptance] leads to security.

"Therefore, each of you must put off falsehood and speak truthfully to his neighbor, for we are all members of one body."
– Ephesians 4:25

Introduction

Let's be honest. Being authentic around others is not always easy because we all struggle with insecurities. Some of us don't like the way we look; we may feel uncomfortable around people perceived as smarter or more successful; or we may lack the confidence to offer our opinion, especially around those with seemingly "stronger" personalities. If we struggle with being comfortable in our own skin around others, our relationships will tend to be shallow and unfulfilling.

The most worthwhile relationships involve people who can just be themselves without pretending otherwise.

The problem of pretending—not being real with ourselves and others—isn't something new. In the Bible, we can trace the problem of hiding our true selves all the way back to Adam and Eve. They felt shame because of their disobedience to God, but before they really understood what had happened, they covered themselves with fig leaves.

But that's not all the deception that transpired in the Garden of Eden that day! They actually attempted to run and hide from God among the trees, a failed endeavor certainly, yet they discovered something vital: covering up, running away, and hiding didn't help. And it won't help us either. Like Adam and Eve, we'll find that lying only creates more distance between the person we long to be and those we care about.

If we're ever going to experience relationships on the level that God intends, we must fight the tendency to pretend we're someone else. In Ephesians 4:25-32, Paul paints a picture of how authentic relationships should look. Notice the first characteristic Paul mentions. To move toward healthy relationships, Paul says, "Let's be honest." And that's where we'll start.

*"[16] These are the things you are to do: **Speak the truth to each other,** and render true and sound judgment in your courts;"*
—Zechariah 8:16

"A friend is one that knows you as you are, understands where you have been, accepts what you have become, and still, gently allows you to grow."
— William Shakespeare

"Be who you are and say what you feel, because those who mind don't matter, and those who matter don't mind."
— Dr. Seuss

Day 1 - The Problem: Fitting In

*"[19] Consequently, you are no longer foreigners and strangers, but **fellow citizens** with God's people and **also members** of his household . . ."*
— Ephesians 2:19

Read Ephesians 2:19.

Have you ever been in a situation where you felt out of place? Maybe you weren't dressed for the occasion. Maybe you didn't know anyone or even felt ignored. Perhaps people stared at you like you were from another planet. Perhaps it was your first day of school or first day on the job. It could have been at a party, a small-town restaurant, or a church event.

Whatever the occasion, no one likes being an outcast, and our first tendency is to try to "fit in" with our environment. In the body of Christ, God doesn't want any of us to feel like we don't belong. He desires for us all to experience the Christian life in a safe place where belonging and safety are shared qualities among everyone involved.

In the body of Christ, there must first be an atmosphere of acceptance in place if we're ever going to experience authentic relationships.

God desires that we live in such security among other believers that we can identify with Paul in Ephesians 4:25 (NIV): "Therefore each of you must put off falsehood and speak truthfully to his neighbor, for we are all members of one body." Telling the truth doesn't always mean we're required to tell all we know. The level of details depends on the depth of relationship, the level of trust, and whether our sharing is really beneficial. Truth must always be shared in love, not sacrificed for love.

Being real, open, and honest with one another won't happen just anywhere. In the body of Christ, there must first be an atmosphere of acceptance in place if we're ever going to experience authentic relationships. This will take work, but it will be worth it!

"There is a beautiful transparency to honest disciples who never wear a false face and do not pretend to be anything but who they are."
— Brennan Manning

1. When was the last time you experienced what it was like to feel out of place? How did you feel? Did you try to fit in?

2. What do you think it means to "fit in" with your community?

Day 2 - The Goal: Following Jesus

Read Romans 15:5-7.

Authentic relationships won't come easy. Our trust levels must be built up, and our defense mechanisms must be torn down. Courage to be real in front of others must be found. In Romans 15, Paul describes some vital aspects that we need to consider when developing authentic relationships. The primary element is understanding the purpose of why we meet: to encourage one another in following Jesus more devotedly.

*"[5] May the God who gives endurance and encouragement **give you the same attitude of mind toward each other** that Christ Jesus had, [6] so that with one mind and one voice you may glorify the God and Father of our Lord Jesus Christ. [7] Accept one another, then, just as Christ accepted you, in order to bring praise to God."*
— Romans 15:5-7

Read Romans 15:5 again.

When it comes to following Jesus, inauthentic relationships can hinder our progress. Ideally, most Christians want to follow Jesus without feeling the need to pretend, hide, or lie about what's really happening on the inside. Sometimes we're tempted to pretend that we're in perfect fellowship with God. Living the lie that "we have it all together" just makes us more religious and judgmental in the long run. Being in a safe environment—where there is no fear of condemnation—helps those of us who have slowly become superficial and numb to honest living; it helps us take the risk to turn things around.

Living the lie that "we have it all together" just makes us more religious and judgmental in the long run.

1. Why is being vulnerable such a hard risk to take sometimes? What makes it easier?

2. How can you help provide a "safe place" for others who follow Jesus, even though they may look at things differently than you do?

"Friendship is born at that moment when one person says to another: "What! You too? I thought I was the only one."
— C. S. Lewis

3. How does becoming a safe place help build unity in your group and in your church?

Day 3 - The Evidence: Unity

It's good to feel comfortable with Christian friends, but it doesn't mean we are exempt from the need to grow closer or go deeper together. For some, the opportunity to be transparent is immediately embraced, but for others, feeling fully accepted may take longer. Authentic communities must involve those who are slow to judge and quick to offer grace. Transparency requires personal risk, but those who embrace the tension with humility will be rewarded with the blessing of experiencing true unity.

*"6 so that **with one mind and one voice** you may glorify the God and Father of our Lord Jesus Christ."*
— Romans 15:6

Read Romans 15:6.

Why is a safe environment necessary for our spiritual growth? Jesus designed the church to be a place where relational barriers are removed and where unity abounds. Jesus wants us to become "one heart" and develop a spirit of unity where the focus is to follow Him. Becoming a safe person comes, not through being profound, but through being personal. Risking vulnerability allows others the opportunity to connect with us and love us on a heart-level, where it matters most. We may think we have nothing to offer, but sharing our own experiences and extending grace to others can be our most powerful contribution toward building a safe place where everyone feels like they belong.

Becoming a "safe person" comes, not through being profound, but through being personal.

1. Have you ever been in a church or group of Christian friends where it was difficult to fit in? Is being vulnerable with Christians easy or risky for you? If it's risky, what makes it that way?

2. What can you do to create a safe environment for those still a little hesitant to be their "true self" around you?

"In the end, we will remember not the words of our enemies, but the silence of our friends."
— Martin Luther King Jr.

3. How can you encourage your Christian friends in building a safe environment where everyone feels like he or she belongs?

Day 4 - The Standard: Christ's Acceptance of Me

Jesus Christ didn't accept us because we were perfect, but because He wanted to do so. Our sins and mistakes didn't prevent Him from pursuing us with His love. He didn't wait for us to get cleaned up first. He embraced us in the midst of our messiness. Jesus accepts us just as we are, but He loves us too much to leave us the way we are. Beyond the mess, we can be confident that Jesus is creating a masterpiece with our lives.

*"[8] But God **demonstrates his own love for us** in this: While we were still sinners, Christ died for us."*
— Romans 5:8

Read Romans 5:8.

There is a "holy moment" that comes when we realize that God unconditionally loves us. He can't love us any more, and He can't love us any less. Through Jesus' loving sacrifice for us on the cross, God willingly embraces us as His children. We can be in God's family without having to fear being kicked out of the house.

The transformation we experience through Jesus Christ doesn't begin with our own efforts to clean up our lives. Our growth begins with Christ's acceptance of us, dirty rags and all. The acceptance of Christ, though undeserved, is what truly puts our soul at rest, allowing us to experience real life change where we need it most. Without Christ's acceptance, we are still under condemnation, knee deep in our insecurities. With this essential part of our relationship with God in mind, Jesus sets the standard for how we are to accept one another.

If we have freely received Jesus' acceptance, then what right do we have to place conditions and limitations on our acceptance of others?

1. Do you ever struggle with the fact that God loves and accepts you freely and completely? What aspect of God's acceptance of you blows you away?

"Most people need love and acceptance a lot more than they need advice."
— Bob Goff

2. How has God's acceptance of you changed the way you see yourself?

Day 5 - Our Practice: Mutual Acceptance

*"[7] **Accept one another**, then, just as Christ accepted you, in order to bring praise to God."*
— Romans 15:7

Read Romans 15:7.

Within the community of believers, we must continue accepting others like Jesus has accepted us because that is the rich soil in which spiritual growth flourishes. Sincerely receiving others should be the natural overflow of a heart that sincerely receives Christ.

If we have freely received Jesus' acceptance of us, then what right do we have to place conditions and limitations on our acceptance of others? Even with all our weaknesses, faults, and poor decisions, Jesus sticks with us. Because Jesus accepts us even in our worst condition, we don't have a right to turn around and treat someone else with less grace. This doesn't mean we must always come to the same conclusions on everything or ought to ignore others' unhealthy choices. Mutual acceptance, however, allows our focus to stay on following Christ together, while valuing one another's unique qualities and personalities.

Mutual acceptance, however, will allow our focus to stay on following Christ together while valuing one another's unique qualities and personalities.

It's a freeing feeling to know we're all on the same level ground of grace. This kind of support will allow us to find safety within our spiritual community and share our spiritual journey on a deeper level. Knowing we're headed in the same direction with the same calling is what makes following Jesus so attractive and so rewarding.

1. Why is it sometimes difficult for us to accept people "just as they are," baggage and all? How can we fight this temptation to condemn others?

"Don't settle for relationships that require losing your voice, your self-respect or your dignity."
— Christine Caine

2. Is accepting people "just as they are" the same as condoning their behavior? Why or why not?

Group Time: Notes

[Acceptance] leads to security.

There really is a community where you can be accepted, appreciated and be yourself, it may just take a little time and effort to discover it. But, after a while, if you find yourself floating from church to church, from group to group, it's time to ask God and those who know you an important question, "Is it me?"

Group Time - Session 2

Let's Start Talking

The struggle with authenticity doesn't get easier as we grow older!

Our struggle with honesty isn't new. As children, we grew up using lies to cover up the fact that we broke the lamp in the living room or punched our sibling in the gut. As we grew older and fell in love for the first time, we likely turned into someone our friends and family didn't recognize. The struggle with authenticity doesn't get easier as we grow older! It continues as we grow into adulthood, as we enter the workplace and begin competing with our peers and neighbors for success and status.

1. Share a lie you told as a kid that got you into big trouble. What was the punishment or consequences that resulted?

2. How do we struggle as adults with authenticity at home, at work, or in our "Church" circles?

Week in Review

"Courage is what it takes to stand up and speak; courage is also what it takes to sit down and listen."
— Winston Churchill

Take a few minutes and look back through your daily readings. Share with your group what you've learned and any points or questions that stood out to you this week.

Group Time - Session 2

Let's Bring It Home

You and I were never meant to live the way of Jesus alone. We need each other more than we may recognize.

Acceptance simply says, "I welcome you."

We must learn to accept one another with love and understanding in the fullest and deepest sense, just as Jesus Christ did for us. Fear, insecurity, and being overly self-conscious will deny your community the "wow" of authenticity you so deeply desire and spiritually need. By the same token, God will become real to "outsiders" when they see real unity demonstrated among "insiders" (John 17:21).

Acceptance simply says, "I welcome you."

Acceptance is first demonstrated through listening. It's not just waiting until others quit talking so you can share your response, but hearing what their hearts are "really" trying to say. When someone puts his or her heart out there, be affirming. A secure person knows how to respond in love without being argumentative or hurtful.

*"[21] that all of them may be one, Father, just as you are in me and I am in you. May they also be in us **so that the world may believe that you have sent me.**"*
— John 17:21

1. Why do some people have an overwhelming need to make others agree with them before acceptance is offered?

2. How can you respect the individuality of others, even if you think their perspectives are wrong?

For the "extroverts" — Don't hold people hostage to your point of view.

"While extroverts are verbal processors, who speak as they think, introverts need to think before we speak."
— Michaela Chung

People are more eager to engage in civil conversation with you rather than divisive debate. Responses without respect are repulsive to everybody. The insecure person finds it easier to pursue being right than pursue being reciprocal in relationships. Consequently,

Group Time - Session 2

"If you do not tell the truth about yourself you cannot tell it about other people." — Virgina Wolfe

we shouldn't ignore truth for the sake of being liked by others, but creating a false sense of moral superiority if things aren't interpreted our way will only lead to greater division without the foundation of mutual acceptance.

1. How might people's hesitation to speak up reflect how they feel about themselves or how they feel about the group?

2. How might a person respectfully disagree with others on an issue without creating division in the relationship?

The security to speak up comes from knowing Jesus accepts you. Security invites transparency.

For the "introverts" — Quit biting your lip.

Stop sinking down in your chair when it's your turn to get involved in the conversation. The security to speak up comes from knowing Jesus accepts you. You are sure to find safe refuge among those in your community as well because they want to show proof that they have accepted you, too. So start speaking up, don't be afraid to be real and begin sharing your life. "Faking it" will just lead to more insecurity, more fear and more hiding. Healing can come to your soul even through a simple confession of how hard it is to open up with others (James 5:16). You may be surprised at the grace you receive as well as the grace you bless others with in the process. Break the cycle. Take a step. You'll be glad you did.

*"[16] Therefore **confess your sins to each other and pray for each other so that you may be healed.** The prayer of a righteous person is powerful and effective." — James 5:16*

1. From your perspective, what does it look like when a person demonstrates acceptance toward you? What makes you feel secure and open to deeper relationship with others?

2. What can you share with your group as a first step towards transparency and honest conversation?

My Response - Session 2

My Prayer Needs:

My Groups Prayer Needs:

"Speak in such a way that others love to listen to you. Listen in such a way that others love to speak to you."
— Anonymous

My Next Step:

Make Up Quickly with Others.

How can we make sure that our anger doesn't slowly infect our hearts and drive a wedge between our relationships?

[Restoration] leads to healing.

"'In your anger do not sin': Do not let the sun go down while you are still angry, and do not give the devil a foothold."

– Ephesians 4:26-27

Introduction

Our feelings of anger are a signal to us that we really DO care what's going on, but they're also a sign that our own selfish motives are getting in the way. Not all anger is sinful, but one aim of authentic community is helping prevent anger from arising in the first place.

"Conflict can only happen if there is something in common."
— Ronald Wopereis

When people start getting honest, things can start getting a little messy. For some, the awkwardness of learning to speak up can lack a gracious filter and turn personal without warning. As people begin to express what they really think, their slant on certain matters can hit a nerve, push buttons, or offend. In the process of sharing our hearts, we can unintentionally hurt others. We may genuinely love and accept each other, but we can find it hard to get along at times.

Our desire for authentic community may not be working out the way we expected, making it uncomfortable or even unbearable. Our lack of experience and understanding in pursuit of honest relationships can push toxic expectations to the surface and add to the tension. As individuals discover the freedom to be their true selves, everyone may not fully appreciate their every expression.

"Honesty and vulnerability endear us to people; they don't endanger us in our relationship."
— Max Lucado

As with any relationship, there is a greater risk of bumping into differences and stepping on egos the closer we get to matters of the heart.

Ignoring even the smallest trace of anger can land us in real trouble. It takes wisdom and maturity to be angry without becoming sinful in our attitudes and actions toward others. Anger can fuel a quick-tempered person to say and do some really hurtful things. It can also entice the mild-tempered person to revert back to disguised judgment and passive condemnation. Both can greatly damage the level of acceptance being built. We need to deal with our anger, not to be proven right but to reconcile in a healthy, godly way with those with whom we're angry.

"Anger, if not restrained, is frequently more hurtful to us than the injury that provokes it."
— Seneca

Day 1 - Look for the Root

The fireworks begin when our desires clash with those of others. We have to look beyond the "fruit" to the "root" of the issue. The health of our relationship with God is revealed in the health of our relationships with others. How we deal with conflict, tension, and frustration reveals the true condition of our heart and the genuineness of our faith. If our love can't go very wide, then it isn't very deep.

"7-10 So let God work his will in you. Yell a loud no to the Devil and watch him scamper. Say a quiet yes to God and he'll be there in no time. Quit dabbling in sin. Purify your inner life. Quit playing the field. Hit bottom, and cry your eyes out. The fun and games are over. Get serious, really serious. Get down on your knees before the Master; it's the only way you'll get on your feet."
— James 4:7-10 (MSG)

Read James 4:7-10.

The Holy Spirit can stir up outrage in us when we experience some form of discrimination, immorality, or bias, but "righteous anger" is defensible only when it relates to problems, not people. Honestly, everyone feels like his or her anger is legitimate, but the reason Scripture discourages us from continuing in anger is because it's rooted in selfishness and in our personal struggle to embrace living God's way. The problem may not be what first comes to mind and may take time to identify and resolve, but getting to the root of the issue can help us think clearly, begin healing, and keep our composure when the situation arises again.

1. Which one of the four areas below is most often the source of your anger?

"In a controversy, the instant we feel anger we have already ceased striving for the truth, and have begun striving for ourselves."
— Thomas Carlyle

The four main areas of our soul where anger emerges:
hurt (a wounded heart)
injustice (a violated right)
fear (a threatened future)
frustration (an unacceptable performance)

2. Why is it easier to point our anger at people instead of our own heart where the real problem lies?

Day 2 - Humble Yourself

At the heart of the issue lies an illuminating reality: our anger stems from our being unfulfilled in our circumstances with other people or even with ourselves. God's grace presents everyone with a new and greater potential, but we can become arrogant and lose our ability to be authentic when we try to find fulfillment in all the wrong places.

"Angry people want you to see how powerful they are... loving people want you to see how powerful YOU are."
— Chief Red Eagle

Nowhere else are lofty expectations piled on individuals like in Christian circles, especially when it comes to spiritual performance and pleasing others. Unlike people do, God never uses guilt or condemnation as a motivator for change. Only selfish, hurting people go about it that way. God doesn't need anything from us in order to be fulfilled, but we desperately need everything He has to offer. He is the only One who has the ability to fulfill all our needs, and no human being will ever fill His shoes. Thankfully, He wants to show us a better way . . . .

Read James 4:7.

*"[7] **Submit yourselves, then, to God.** Resist the devil, and he will flee from you."*
— James 4:7

Religious experiences and Bible knowledge can give us a false sense of moral superiority and can actually lead to greater division when pride gets in the way. We can be tempted to play an internal game of "hide and seek" with friends and especially with God. Submitting ourselves to God is the first step in removing our ego from the equation as we seek to offer an honest response that honors Him, despite the friction. When it comes to conflict, He asks us to go first, no matter what the other person chooses to do.

Submitting ourselves to God is the first step in removing our ego from the equation as we seek to offer an honest response that honors Him despite the friction.

1. In what ways is it actually more damaging to pretend there is no conflict in our relationships when, in fact, there really is?

2. How can we demonstrate humility and love in a genuine way towards a person before we begin addressing the conflict we are experiencing with him or her?

Day 3 - Don't Fall for the Trap

"[7] Submit yourselves, then, to God. ***Resist the devil, and he will flee from you."***
— James 4:7

Read James 4:7b.

Staying in the right frame of mind can be tough, especially when emotions run high. Satan would love nothing more than to divide Christians and turn them against each other. Rejection is one of Satan's greatest weapons to corrupt relationships within God's family. Instead of asking us to reject people, God calls us to reject the lies of our greatest enemy. Learning how to "stay in love" with people when negative emotions arise is vital to resisting what the devil wants to destroy.

Rejection is one of Satan's greatest weapons used to corrupt relationships within God's family.

Be patient. Not everyone is at the same place or walks the same pace on his or her journey with Christ. Some long-time followers of Jesus may not really know how to love people like you would expect them to do. For others, their Christian experience has never led them to a deeper understanding of grace for themselves, much less how to offer it to others. Remember, Satan is our enemy, not our community. Those who resist Satan's trap will retain a gentle heart that can humbly offer grace to those in need and will help everyone avoid a dangerous pitfall.

1. What temptation are you most often vulnerable to when you become angry? *(For example, do you tend to protect your reputation, control others, gossip, play the victim, manipulate through gifts, seek pleasure, give in to an addiction, isolate yourself from others, etc.?)*

"Conflict cannot survive without your participation."
— Wayne Dyer

2. How can you resolve the problem without rejecting the person?

Day 4 - Open Your Heart to God Daily

If we're to deal with tension in a healthy way, we have to confront ourselves before confronting others. Maturity is first taking responsibility for what we bring to the table. It's dealing with "me" before I deal with "we."

Read James 4:8a.

*"[8] **Come near to God and he will come near to you.** Wash your hands, you sinners, and purify your hearts, you double-minded."*
— James 4:8

Taking responsibility for resolving conflict begins with drawing closer to God personally. We become more intimate with Him when we humble our heart toward Him. Drawing near to God is not about doing more religious activity but about dealing with the real issues below the surface. It's getting honest before God about what's going on in our heart and facing the real issue that is stirring anger in us.

No one has the power to make us angry. Becoming angry is a choice we make. Though past and present circumstances may play a role, the real battle lies not outside but within. God wants us to draw close to Him, not so He can shame us but to heal us from the inside out. The more we're exposed to the loving heart of God, the healthier our responses will be toward others.

Maturity is taking responsibility. It's dealing with me before I deal with "we."

1. Why is it so important to confront ourselves first before we confront others?

2. How do our past experiences affect our present relationships, both positively and negatively?

3. What does it mean to process conviction in a healthy way? How do we navigate the emotions that may come as a result of conviction without shaming ourselves in the process?

"Until we can receive with an open heart, we are never really giving with an open heart."
— Brene' Brown

Day 5 - Stay Clean

It's vital that we become aware of how God wants to change the way we respond, transforming us from the inside out. Instead of focusing on Satan's schemes, we need to give our attention to Scripture and the guidance it offers for a true change of heart that can render Satan powerless before any damage is done.

"8 Come near to God and he will come near to you. ***Wash your hands****, you sinners, and* ***purify your hearts****, you double-minded."*
— James 4:8

Read James 4:8b.

We can't manufacture the kind of change that God can bring in our life and the lives of others. Like we discussed earlier, anger really is a sign that we care, but we usually minimize the early warnings by calling them concerns, frustrations, or "being a little upset." We don't recognize when we're getting angry. When unaware of our anger level, we can create a great deal of collateral damage. Maturity calls us to be proactive and know when our responses might communicate something different than what our hearts intend. People will know if our heart is full of judgment or grace by our delivery and how we follow up.

"Hurt is a feeling that calls us to healing, not resentment."
— Chip Dodd

1. What physical, emotional, or spiritual symptoms do you experience when you have unresolved anger?

Physical—*high blood pressure, stomach pain, headaches, insomnia, compulsive eating/drinking/exercising/working, etc.?*
Emotional—*anxiety, bitterness, compulsiveness, depression, fear, insecurity, phobias, worry, etc.?*
Spiritual—*loss of faith, energy, confidence, freedom, sensitivity, vision, perspective, identity, etc.?*

"How much more grievous are the consequences of anger than the causes of it."
— Marcus Aurelius

2. How can understanding the symptoms around your response to anger help keep you from hurting others? Why is it important to follow up quickly with others when we do cause hurt?

Group Time: Notes

[Restoration] leads to healing.

"Anger is the most impotent of passions. It effects nothing it goes about, and hurts the one who is possessed by it more than the one against whom it is directed."
— Carl Sandburg

Group Time - Session 3

Let's Start Talking

"Whenever you're in conflict with someone, there is one factor that can make the difference between damaging your relationship and deepening it. That factor is attitude."
— William James

Community is ripe for conflict. As in a marriage, we start out with great dreams and can be a little idealistic about how our relationships are going to turn out. Then reality sets in. With the first indication of differing personalities and opinions, the tension and frustration levels begin to rise. Some people are inclined to shut up, cover up, blow up, or pack up, even in the slightest disagreement. Disagreements are inevitable, but conflict can actually help make our relationships stronger. How we deal with our differences will make all the difference.

1. What's one of the most ridiculous things you've ever gotten angry about?

2. Are you inclined to shut up, cover up, blow up, or pack up when you get angry? Do you wear your emotions on your sleeve, avoid conflict at all costs, or do something in between? Would your family or friends agree with your answer?

"Every expression of anger is the tragic expression of an unmet need."
— Marshall B. Rosenberg

Week in Review

Take a few minutes to look back through your daily readings. Share with your group what you've learned and any points or questions that stood out to you this week.

"When there is an elephant in the room, introduce him."
— Unknown

Group Time - Session 3

Let's Bring It Home

If you sense that others have been angry with you, don't wait on them to come to you. Take the first step out of love for them and because you value the relationship.

Reconciliation simply says, "I value you."

How we deal with anger is a direct reflection of how we've experienced grace. Pride says, "I have the right to be angry." Grace says, "I lay down my right to be angry."

Reconciliation simply says, "I value you."

Creating expectations can be a good thing, but they need to be done God's way and on His timetable. We must learn to love others where they are, for who they are, and as they are, just like Jesus did for us. Forgiven people forgive people. Healed people heal people. Loved people love people. Graced people grace people. What we've received from God will be revealed in how we respond to others.

Procrastination is the enemy of authentic relationships.

1. When can expectations be a healthy thing? When can they be unhealthy?

2. How can we be intentional about loving someone where they are without compromising who we are?

*"[1] What causes fights and quarrels among you? Don't they come from **your desires that battle within** you?"*
— James 4:1

Don't wait . . . Look inside first!

Reconciliation depends on an honest look inside. The first step is humbly admitting and sorting out our own selfish judgments before we choose to engage or separate ourselves from the person with whom we feel tension. The problem may actually stem from a gap in maturity, a shallow perspective, or a personality issue on our part that

Group Time - Session 3

needs to be examined. Loving people who are different from us can be challenging, but acknowledging and owning up to our faults can revive the freedom of honest conversation and restore our heart toward those we're called to love.

"I'm not in this world to live up to your expectations and you're not in this world to live up to mine."
— Bruce Lee

1. What level of relationship should we be expected to develop with those with whom we have little in common?

2. When should distance be allowable in a relationship? When should it not be?

Don't wait . . . Love goes first!

If you sense that someone is angry with you, take the first step and go to him or her first with a humble, loving heart. Whether engaging with family members, friends, or others in life, communicate up front that you care about them and value the relationship. Let them know your heart is to reconcile any differences and work out the problem that has come between you.

"The beginning of love is to let those we love be perfectly themselves, and not twist them to fit our own image. Otherwise we love only the reflection of ourselves we find in them."
— Thomas Merton

Procrastination is the enemy of authentic relationships. We need to quickly move from what has brought about the hostility to how we can bring the situation to a loving conclusion for the glory of God and the good of others. Getting angry gives proof we are human, but resolving anger gives proof that we are following Jesus and love our friends.

1. With whom do you need to make things right with before you go to bed tonight?

2. What expectations do you have of someone else that needs to be released to God for now?

My Response - Session 3

My Prayer Needs:

My Groups Prayer Needs:

"People, even more than things, have to be restored, renewed, revived, reclaimed, and redeemed; never throw out anyone."
— Audrey Hepburn

My Next Step:

Step Up
and Do My Part.

How can we begin building trust with others and continue to demonstrate that we are a trustworthy person?

[Trust] leads to intimacy.

"He who has been stealing must steal no longer, but must work, doing something useful with his own hands, that he may have something to share with those in need."
– Ephesians 4:28

Introduction

One of the most important qualities for building healthy community is interdependence, a mutual reliance on one another for needed support. When we're given the opportunity to meet a need in someone's life in a responsible and honest way, we're building trust.

"Whoever is careless with the truth in small matters cannot be trusted with important matters."
— Albert Einstein

In order to feel connected on a deeper level, we must pursue trusting each other and, most importantly, become trustworthy ourselves.

We can lose our intentionality and become lazy when it comes to investing in the lives of others. Building trust requires that we live with integrity and do our share of the work in developing relationships. The more open a person becomes, the greater the responsibility we have in holding up our end of the deal.

The balance of community is to love others and be loved, to serve others and be served, to know others and be known. Healthy community allows everyone to develop a maturing passion for giving as well as receiving. We can become "robbers" and "users" of community when we only participate for our own benefit, adding nothing in return. Self-centeredness is a remnant of the "old person" we used to be, not the new person we are in Christ.

"But it is impossible to go through life without trust; that is to be imprisoned in the worst cell of all, oneself."
— Graham Greene

Instead of focusing on being "ministered to," followers of Jesus create opportunities for ministry to others. Our relationships must reach the place where we give and replenish each other's lives, not only take and deplete. This mutual refreshment of one another is a sign that we're living as a new person in Christ, leaving our old life and the world's way of living behind.

Trust grows the more we show ourselves to be trustworthy. We must go beyond the focus of what we can gain from community to what we bring into it. In the end, this is where we discover a higher purpose and greater fulfillment than we could have ever imagined.

"Few delights can equal the mere presence of one whom we trust utterly."
— George MacDonald

Day 1 - Be Consistent

Integrity is a way of life. It's not an option for us to pick and choose. Either we have it or we don't. It's demonstrated in how reliable we are, regardless of how big or small the situation may be in our eyes. Trust demands that our words match our actions. As we experience a deeper sense of acceptance among those in our community, the more talking we will do. But if what we say outweighs how we live, we lose trust.

*" [10] **Whoever can be trusted with very little can also be trusted with much**, and whoever is dishonest with very little will also be dishonest with much."*
— Luke 16:10

Read Luke 16:10.

Trust requires a track record. It takes evidence to earn credibility and time to build a reputation as a trustworthy person. It takes consistency to draw a following because "seeing is believing." Trustworthy people become magnets for those whom God is leading to a safe place for life-change.

All of us can find excuses for missing our time together or leverage another opportunity as more important, but reoccurring excuses for our lack of involvement, even in the smallest things, reveal an unhealthy attitude toward our community—an indication that we've lost sight of how God is using us to make a difference in the lives of others. Consistency is the foundational measurement of our integrity. It demonstrates to our community that they can rely on us and that our friendship is important. When we give our word, all who know us can be totally confident that our actions will back it up.

"Men trust their ears less than their eyes."
— Herodotus

1. What are some important aspects of community that need consistency?

2. What past track records make the hurdle of mistrust hard to overcome?

"It's not what we do once in a while that shapes our lives. It's what we do consistently."
— Tony Robbins

3. What are some things we should be willing to sacrifice for our community in order to demonstrate our commitment to it?

Day 2 - Realize What's at Stake

As we commit ourselves to becoming trustworthy, we're also proving ourselves to be worthy of the deeper responsibilities and delicate tasks within our community. It requires consistency as well as true compassion, taking seriously the need to express empathy and concern for others who've placed their hearts on the line.

Read Luke 16:11.

"[11] So if you have not been trustworthy in handling worldly wealth, ***who will trust you with true riches?***"
— *Luke 16:11*

All of us have been wounded on some level, but some have endured spiritual, emotional, mental, or physical abuse in ways most of us can't fathom. "Trust" isn't a flippant buzz word for them; it's a matter of life or death for their soul's survival. No amount of virtuous pressure will quickly demolish the fortress around their heart, and for good reason.

Parker Palmer shares from his book, A *Hidden Wholeness*, that the soul slams shut the moment someone attempts to fix it, rescue it, or advise it. Our soul craves to be witnessed, heard, received, and honored. That's all. Most of the time, we already know what to do. We just need a safe environment with a great deal of listening, little talking, and freedom from the fear of gossip. Being present without trying to counsel or repair someone's brokenness while preserving his or her dignity is the first priority of healthy community and the highest privilege God has given us.

"Friendship is the inexpressible comfort of feeling safe with a person, having neither to weigh thoughts or measure words."
— George Eliot

In order for a heart to remain open, we must tenderly and patiently engage with honest, open questions with the goal of genuine understanding, not the delivery of advice in disguise. The first steps toward recovery may depend on the person's ability to trust us for the tender compassion their soul desperately needs for healing to begin.

"Trust is not an obsession, it's an extension of love. When we truly love someone, we give them our heart to hold in their hands. And when that love is returned, that very trust is balm to our souls."
— Julie Lessman

1. How do you respond when someone gives you insight into a particular hurt in his or her life? Are you prone to listen, lecture, or gossip later? Why?

2. When is the appropriate time and the best way to offer advice?

Day 3 - Prove It

Trust is proven through our work. Work doesn't end when *we* are done but when the *job* is done. God calls us to serve the needs of others until utter exhaustion or weariness if necessary. It's the picture of taking a beating for the cause of someone else. If we follow Jesus' example, we must never give up on others because He will never give up on us.

"[2] Now it is required that those who have been given a trust ***must prove faithful.****"*
— 1 Corinthians 4:2

Read 1 Corinthians 4:2.

God isn't demanding that we be successful, but that we prove faithful. We need effort, work, and "follow through" on our part, but we can leave the results up to Him. Our trust is going to be tested, especially when the results don't develop like expected. We have to keep going, even through disappointment.

"We judge ourselves by our intentions and others by their behavior."
— Stephen M. R. Covey

Jesus has given us grace and trusts us to use it on behalf of others. More important than our expectations, God's reputation is at hand. Even in the midst of suffering the consequences of others' mistakes and misunderstandings, we need to continue responding with the love and kindness we've been given by Jesus. When we truly understand grace, we're patient with others, even when things get messy; we continue holding them in high regard and loving them through the worst of times. It gives evidence that God's grace is working through us and that we're committed to His greater purpose of restoration.

"Friendship isn't about who you've known the longest. It's about who walked into your life, said 'I'm here for you' and proved it."
— Unknown

1. If God would make you the standard of faithfulness for your community, what would it look like?

2. What should a group be willing to do in earning back the trust of someone who feels burned or fearful of deeper engagement?

Day 4 - Be Devoted

We used to live in certain ways before we came to know Jesus Christ and His transforming grace. If He is in us, He will change us. The way we live and the way we love will reflect the change He's bringing on the inside.

"[8] This is a trustworthy saying. And I want you to stress these things, so that those who have trusted in God may be careful ***to devote themselves*** *to doing what is good. These things are excellent and profitable for everyone."*
— Titus 3:8

Read Titus 3:8.

Being trustworthy requires us to engage our lives with others in our community. If we're not willing to put our heart into it, we should never expect it of others. The unengaged are unattractive to those seeking authenticity and can't be trusted to have the best interest of the group in mind. Authentic community requires that everyone engage with passion and have some skin in the game. Community is not a spectator sport. Everyone must be willing to participate like we're "all in."

It goes without saying, but we must remember that we're all imperfect and will stumble in our attempts to be trustworthy. It's vital that we think the best of each other and give each other the opportunity to learn and recover from a mistake. When our heart is tender toward God, it will help us keep our hearts tender toward each other when we have a humbling moment of humanity.

Everyone must be willing to participate like we're "all in."

We benefit the lives of others the most when we keep going and keep growing. Trusting in God will be evident by how we give our life away to others. What has become yours is not just for you. You are blessed to be a blessing and must keep developing your heart and investing your life so you'll have something to offer others on their journey.

"Not surprisingly, the place we're most likely to experience testing is exactly where we struggle most to trust God."
— Bruce Wilkinson

1. What would change about your relationships if you lived like they owed you nothing?

2. When can our assumptions about others do more harm than good?

Day 5 - Focus On The Essentials

What we believe is intimately connected to our heart. In helping to guide others to right beliefs, we care for each person's heart, all in partnership with our conviction for God's truth. Scripture is meant to bring life and create conversation, not discouragement and division. We can have great knowledge of Scripture and honor for it but still exude spiritual immaturity in how we use it.

*"[9] But **avoid foolish controversies and genealogies and arguments and quarrels** about the law, because these are unprofitable and useless." — Titus 3:9*

Read Titus 3:9.

It takes discipline and work to obey the standards given to us in God's Word. We must be willing to line up our lives with the truth of Scripture in order to truly follow Jesus. When we honor God's Word with our lives, it lets those around us know we can be depended on to see the needs of our community in a beneficial way through the lens of the Bible.

Trust is diverted when people discover that we have an agenda above the benefit and good of others. Those who are immature and insecure will be tempted to overreact to unfiltered statements instead of creating healthy, redemptive, truth-centered conversation. We must stay focused on the main ideas of Scripture and not get caught up in self-righteous expression and spiritual vanity that actually distract us from real life-change.

"To be trusted is a greater compliment than being loved." — George MacDonald

It's great that we read Scripture, but we must let Scripture read us. May we be committed to discuss it for our good and respond to it for God's glory.

1. How can you challenge what someone believes without it coming across in a condemning way?

"Show respect even to people who don't deserve it; not as a reflection of their character, but as a reflection of yours." — Dave Willis

2. What's the best way to deal with side issues or address specific controversies without creating unnecessary division in the group?

Group Time: Notes

[Trust] leads to intimacy.

"People grow when they are loved well. If you want to help others heal, love them without an agenda."
— Mike McHargue

Group Time - Session 4

Let's Start Talking

Whom we trust and the depth of that trust is evident by what we're willing to share with them. Think about whom you would lend your car to, rely on to meet a deadline, or let keep your kids overnight. With whom would you share a family secret or confess a huge personal mistake? We've figured out that there are some people we wouldn't want to tell how much we spent on our favorite jeans, who we invited over for dinner last weekend, where we went on vacation, or what's in our refrigerator. It's comforting to know those whom we can trust and a little disheartening to know those whom we wouldn't. Once we've been burned by someone breaking trust, it can be hard to recover and get back to normal. But in spite of the risk, there's plenty of evidence that it can be done.

When you make a commitment, you build hope. When you keep your commitment, you build trust.

1. Tell about the experience when you learned that Santa Claus doesn't really exist. (Maybe it's right now.)

2. Who was the first person you remember as being trustworthy? What made you trust this person?

"Peace and trust take years to build and seconds to shatter."
— Mahogany SilverRain

3. Describe an experience that required you to take a huge leap of faith. What made it feel risky? Was it worth it?

Week in Review

Take a few minutes to look back through your daily readings. Share with your group what you've learned and any points or questions that stood out to you this week.

Group Time - Session 4

Let's Bring It Home

Trust is the foundation on which genuine relationships must be built and is the bridge to lasting, fulfilling community, where honest appreciation for others is revealed through intentional action.

Trust simply says, "I'll invest with you."

Trust can be developed only in a safe place among safe people where the value of each person is continually reinforced. An unsafe atmosphere can leave people feeling vulnerable and exploited with no desire to engage their hearts with us again. People will revert back to hiding, pretending, and lying when the risk of trust is too great.

Trust simply says, "I'll invest with you."

Trust is proven and cultivated through our actions.

Breaking trust can inflict new damage on old wounds and reaffirm a person's struggle of feeling unworthy of love, respect, and value. Mistrust is not easily cleared from our conscious and can take a long time to be rebuilt, making the relationship awkward when trust is in doubt. When trust is broken, words lose their meaning. Only positive experiences will communicate a change of heart.

"Character is not created in isolation or repose; it's forged through interaction with others and the world."
— David Corbett

1. In what ways might a small group encourage or discourage trust?

2. When is isolation from others natural and necessary? When is it harmful and hurtful?

"The place of isolation can become the place of revelation."
— Steven Furtick

Don't be a community kleptomaniac!

It's not about what we get but what we give that demonstrates our maturity and love for people. There are seasons in community when our individual needs can be overwhelming and require a great amount of attention. But when our needs are being met and we continue to

Group Time - Session 4

"God has given us two hands--one to receive with and the other to give with. We are not cisterns made for hoarding; we are channels made for sharing."
— Billy Graham

take, the Bible calls this stealing. One way we can rob our community is by dominating the group's attention for ourselves without regard for helping others to engage, share, and be ministered to effectively. We must be aware of when the opportunity to be heard enables us to hoard the group's attention in an unhealthy way. Some of us may not be deliberately taking from the community, but by bringing nothing to it, we are still robbing. Any excuse for remaining neutral restricts the development of trust.

1. When is it unhealthy to give someone more or less attention?

2. What can your group do to give everyone the opportunity to be engaged, share, and be ministered to effectively?

Create positive experiences.

We have the choice to fill in questionable moments with either trust or suspicion. The more positive experiences we have with others, the more likely the gap will be filled with trust during times of uncertainty. A lack of self-awareness, undeveloped people skills, or an abrasive personality can inhibit others from trusting us. Some of us may be great at entertaining a roomful of people but less than great at engaging others on a heart level. Don't be offended if those who desire a deeper relationship with us hold back trust until they have enough evidence to the contrary.

"Trust is the fruit of a relationship in which you know you are loved."
— William P. Young

1. What behaviors allow us to build trust or lead us to be suspicious?

2. What can you do individually or as a group to demonstrate your desire to be trustworthy this week?

My Response - Session 4

My Prayer Needs:

My Groups Prayer Needs:

"[3] When I am afraid, I put my trust in you. [4] In God, whose word I praise—in God I trust and am not afraid. What can mere mortals do to me?"
— Psalm 56:3-4

My Next Step:

Build Up
with My Words.

How can we express our belief in others with the words we speak and demonstrate that we have his or her best interest in mind?

[Encouragement] leads to confidence.

"Do not let any unwholesome talk come out of your mouths, but only what is helpful for building others up according to their needs, that it may benefit those who listen."
– Ephesians 4:29

Introduction

One of the greatest benefits of community is experiencing uplifting conversation. As we develop a heart for one another and begin looking for ways to meet one another's needs, we'll discover encouragement as one of the most important gifts we all could use in more abundance.

Words are small, but they hold great potential. Jesus lets us see the power of words when He spoke the universe into existence, declared forgiveness to sinners, pronounced healing to the sick, granted deliverance from the demonic, and revealed grace through His kingdom. By design, our words are one of the most powerful tools that God gives us and include a wide range of uses that can build up or destroy with little or no effort.

"Our chief want is someone who will inspire us to be what we know we could be."
— Ralph Waldo Emerson

Scripture powerfully illustrates the strength of our speech. Like a horse's bit tames its wild nature and a rudder directs a ship amidst opposing seas, the smallest word can make great impact.

We must fight against the negative forces at work in and around us that will influence our words in a direction we don't want them to go. The ability to keep our mouth under control will affect our entire lives, including those who come under the influence of our words. Words wrongly used can ruin a relationship, perpetuate a false reality, tarnish a reputation, and wound the souls of those who give ear to what we say. How we speak reveals our spiritual health on the inside as well as our heart for our friends.

The smallest word can make great impact.

God invites us to join Him in what He's doing—building others up to empower them where they need it most.

What rolls off the tongue is either helpful or harmful to God's cause. Jesus granted us the authority and power to bring life or death with every word spoken. God desires that we use our words to make a positive contribution, but how we use them is our choice alone to make.

"Instruction does much, but encouragement everything."
— Johann Wolfgang von Goethe

Day 1 - Purpose to Praise

Part of maintaining a safe environment for healthy relationships to flourish is being aware of what's going on, not only in the hearts of others but, most importantly, in our own. Authenticity calls us to take personal responsibility for our own responses. Our job is to take the lead in making sure our heart is in good condition and to trust that others will follow our example and do the same.

"45 A good man brings good things out of the good stored up in his heart, and an evil man brings evil things out of the evil stored up in his heart. ***For the mouth speaks what the heart is full of."***
— Luke 6:45

Read Luke 6:45.

Praising and cursing are a contradiction in purpose. Praise declares truth and brings life. Cursing declares lies and brings death. Words are powerful. They have the capacity to reach deep into our hearts and change everything. Just like the Word of God can "divide our soul," so can the words we speak.

Unwholesome talk is filled with "rotten" words that are repulsive to the Holy Spirit and can destroy what God is building in us. Cursing is not natural to who we are in Christ and is an unacceptable end for those who claim to follow Jesus.

"The chief purpose of life, for any of us, is to increase according to our capacity our knowledge of God by all means we have, and to be moved by it to praise and thanks."
— J. R. R. Tolkien

This is so true: The moment we placed our faith in Jesus Christ, we were supernaturally transformed by the Holy Spirit into a new creation with a new heart for a new purpose. When the wellspring of our heart is overflowing with the grace and life of Jesus, truth and praise will spill out into every conversation for the good of all who hear.

1. What was your last conversation like with a "life-giving" friend, when you felt loved and alive through what he or she said to you?

2. When and where are you most tempted to use "rotten" words and engage in destructive conversation? With others? With yourself?

Day 2 - Help Others Grow

When our community gets together, each one of us has the awesome opportunity to be an encourager. The ability to encourage others is an incredible privilege and an important task. We must show high regard for what we offer in the way of instruction. The critical nature of guiding people gives us a great responsibility we shouldn't take lightly.

"[3] Do nothing out of selfish ambition or vain conceit. Rather, in humility ***value others above yourselves,*** *[4] not looking to your own interests but* ***each of you to the interests of the others."***
— Philippians 2:3-4

Read Philippians 2:3-4.

When spoken, words have the ability to bind or loosen things in our hearts (Matt. 18:18). The challenge of edification is to speak biblically about one another and use words that edify and support what God says about us. True edification calls more attention to a person's gifts than gaps. It encourages and empowers others to do the right thing with the right heart.

The best motives place what others need above our own. Our mandate is to speak only what will benefit each person's spiritual progress. The wisdom and experiences we pass along should be offered without obligation, even when we think we have some great things to say. Our approach with others should show we're taking responsibility with them, not from them. It's what we would want to experience if we were in their shoes.

"If you don't go out on the limb, you'll miss out on the fruit."
— Dan Cathy

The goal of listening is more than understanding; it's making people feel understood. When people know they truly matter to you, your words will matter even more to them. Never be surprised by the power of an encouraging word and how others will want to live up to it.

1. Why is it important for you to be actively involved in sharing knowledge and experience with others in your community?

"You should show encouragement whenever you can. People try harder when they know that someone cares about them."
— Stephanie Perkins

2. What does it look like to offer encouragement and instruction with someone without taking responsibility for the outcome?

Day 3 - Make a Timely Investment

Different seasons require different words. It takes discernment to know the real need below the surface and where the Holy Spirit is at work. What we say needs to always be full of grace so our friends can walk away with the best answer.

"[6] Let your conversation be always full of grace, seasoned with salt, ***so that you may know how to answer everyone."***
— Colossians 4:6

Read Colossians 4:6.

Most of us worry more about *what* to answer instead of *how* to answer. Our head won't receive what our hearts can't accept. It's more than what's spoken; it's how we speak. The focus is not on what we have to offer, but what others need to hear in the moment. Just because a thought comes to mind doesn't mean it should come out of our mouth. If they don't need it, don't say it.

Having a rich history of relationship offers insight into the best way to respond to others and how others may respond to what we say. Redemptive conversations can become harder the longer we've known a person. Though past encounters can help us interpret a better approach, we must be careful in how we bring these into the process. Responding with grace can help others receive with grace.

Edification doesn't inflict pain but infuses grace and undergirds a person's ability to obey God. Acknowledge problems but elevate possibilities. Let your words instill courage and hope, helping others believe they can do whatever God has called them to do.

"At the beginning, you say things you need to say. As time passes, you learn to say what others need to hear."
— Dan Rockwell

1. When can having a long history of friendship be a benefit during deep conversations? When can it be a barrier?

2. When is it helpful to bring up past situations? When can it be harmful in the moment?

Day 4 - Add Value

One of the greatest opportunities we have with those in our lives is to add value to theirs. It's essential to bring significance as well as assurance right where they need it most.

*"[19] Let us therefore **make every effort** to do what leads to **peace and to mutual edification.**"*
— Romans 14:19

Read Romans 14:19.

When someone takes a risk in becoming vulnerable and sharing a need, we need to do all we can to honor his or her trust in us. Compassion is what opens hearts to receive comfort, counsel, and encouragement. It's not time to "lord over them" but elevate them as we would want for ourselves if in the same situation.

Don't forget what it was like the last time we didn't know how to move forward. We needed encouragement to lower our anxiety in the midst of the situation, but we also needed practical advice to know how to change it. Most everyone else will probably feel the same way, too.

"The people who taught me the most didn't think they were my teacher; they just thought we were friends."
— Bob Goff

Truth that encourages can be general to all believers, but tools that equip must be specific to the need. Take time to discover people's motivation, tap into their goals and dreams, help them weigh the costs and benefits, and discover what it takes to get there. It can be as simple as sharing your experience or offering your perspective.

Speak to their need, for who God created them to be, and help them clearly see a next step. Remember that our efforts can help toward improving results and improving our relationship at the same time. We will find it does our heart just as good to know we've built up a friend and empowered him or her for success.

"Be helpful. When you see a person without a smile, give him one of yours."
— Zig Ziglar

1. What's the difference between being encouraged and being equipped?

2. How does compassion help when offering instruction?

Day 5 - Remember Who's Listening

Our conversation should always result in a better understanding of God's grace, both for us and those who hear us. Yet, over time, we can allow lies, unforgiveness, jealousy, gossip, and even our own wounds to pollute our comments. Our inner world of words swirling in our soul can be noticeable and influence those exposed to it. Our words can bring freedom or create strongholds in the hearts of those who grant authority to our voice, so we must pay attention to those who respond to what we convey in our speech.

*"[9] Whatever you have learned or received or **heard from me**, or seen in me—put it into practice. And the God of peace will be with you."*
— Philippians 4:9

Read Philippians 4:9.

Grace is undeserved favor. We may not always feel that others deserve gracious words, but God wants us to extend grace to others the same way He has extended grace to us—undeservedly. Jesus Christ made it possible for every person on the planet to be eternally changed in a moment of grace. As His followers, there is no greater satisfaction than to see God use us to help others connect with Jesus and experience His life-changing grace.

Mutual acceptance, however, will allow our focus to stay on following Christ together while valuing one another's unique qualities and personalities.

Every person on the planet is created in the image of God, so there's something of value we can speak to and build up in every person. The Holy Spirit can help us spot and call out the good things in others. God can use gracious words to make beauty from ashes, convert defeat into victory, and unearth joy in the midst of sorrow. Through our everyday conversations, we can become ambassadors of grace and connect people with our gracious God when we speak from His heart.

"He who speaks evil of an absent man or woman is not welcome at this table."
— Augustine

1. Think about those in your life who are influenced by you. Do you notice gracious talk from those who "listen" to you?

2. What does it mean for our words to "bring freedom or create strongholds" for others? When can either of these be good or bad?

Group Time: Notes

[Encouragement] leads to confidence.

With so much negativity in our world, it's important for us to be involved in a community of people who are committed to helping others follow Jesus well. God wants to build confidence in us through the encouragement we receive from those who have our best interest in mind.

Group Time - Session 5

Let's Start Talking

We've all heard the old saying, "Sticks and stones may break my bones, but words will never hurt me." Perhaps many of us have remembered this phrase right after somebody's words have hurt us, knowing it's not true! Even as children, we understood that words could make us feel really good or really bad and were easily accessible as a first line of defense. As adults, our words are more important now than ever. We still need them to stir up courage within us so we can press on with confidence in our daily lives. It's easy to gravitate toward people who are positive by nature, but finding those who truly believe in us can be worth more than gold!

"Those who are lifting the world upward and onward are those who encourage more than criticize."
— Elizabeth Harrison

1. What one worship song or lyric has God used to speak to your heart this week? What is your greatest taken-away from it?

2. Think of a high-profile person known for encouragement and positivity. Why do you like him or her? Or maybe, why not?

3. What's the most memorable encouragement you've ever received? What's the significance of the person who gave it?

"How would your life be different if...You walked away from gossip and verbal defamation? Let today be the day...You speak only the good you know of other people and encourage others to do the same."
— Steve Maraboli

Week in Review

Take a few minutes to look back through your daily readings. Share with your group what you've learned and any points or questions that stood out to you this week.

Group Time - Session 5

Let's Bring It Home

You and I were made to speak Life into others and help them have the courage to follow Jesus in whatever they're going through.

Encouragement simply says, "I believe in you."

The greatest community experience is one in which everyone believes in each other and has each other's best interests in mind. Most of us have a hard enough time dealing with the tsunami of discouragement and negativity that comes naturally in daily life, and access to this kind of community can provide a refreshing oasis. Encouragement comes through speaking truth and grace in such a way as to build a person up on the inside. It's more than just offering a positive thought; it's helping to develop a truthful mind that can withstand the bombardment of external pressures that try to tear us down.

Encouragement simply says, "I believe in you."

1. Whom do you go out of your way to talk to when you're seeking encouragement and need a boost in confidence? Why?

"Strive not to be a success, but rather to be of value."
— Albert Einstein

2. Why is it important to consistently reinforce our relationship with Jesus, as well as our identity, with promises from Scripture?

For the "truther"—Just because it's right doesn't mean right now.

There are times when the facts should be stated bluntly. But elevating personal justification above a kind, considerate answer can distract the hearer from the truth because of how it's delivered. Remember: Most people struggle through discouragement on an emotional level more than anything else. A "bull in a China closet" does nothing but break things, so be careful where and how you let "truth" loose. Our mandate is to practice building up, not to demolish. A kind answer turns away wrath, and love covers a multitude of sins, so a "biblical" answer requires emotional consideration for the best outcome. Ears don't hear

"Encourage everyone you meet with a smile or compliment. Make them feel better when you leave their presence and they will always be glad to see you coming."
— Joyce Meyer

Group Time - Session 5

Ears don't hear when the heart is closed.

when the heart is closed. If you choose to bruise, you choose to lose. Building someone's confidence requires encouragement behind the words in order to be truly believable.

1. How can "speaking only what is helpful" be a real challenge for those who have knowledge and experience in a particular area? How might it reflect your heart for others by what you leave out?

For the "tender"—Most people are trying to help you, not hurt you.

Let's face it: most of us wear our heart on our sleeve. Expressing our emotions openly can be a great strength, yet we may not always realize how others hear or receive our words, even when we're trying to give encouragement or show empathy. When on the receiving end, we may find it hard to hear the truth when we feel it wasn't spoken in love or with sensitivity. Sometimes our emotional responses don't reflect the intentions behind the delivery of others' communications with us.

"We always see the worst in our selves. Our most vulnerable selves. We need someone to get close enough to tell us that we're wrong. Someone we trust."
— Rachel Cohn

So here's a strategy to consider: Instead of making quick, emotional interpretations of others' words, stop and make an intentional decision to think the best about the person and his or her motive for speaking into your life. If people didn't care, they wouldn't share. Give the Holy Spirit an opportunity to verify the message before you vilify the messenger. Even if you need time to process what was shared, receive it with thankfulness, knowing in the end God will turn it into a blessing no matter what.

1. How can our level of openness to what others say reflect the wounds of our heart more than the heart of their words?

2. Take time to pray for each other and encourage one another through offering spiritual insights, impressions, and Scripture as they come to mind and heart.

My Response - Session 5

My Prayer Needs:

My Groups Prayer Needs:

"Be mindful when it comes to your words. A string of some that don't mean much to you, may stick with someone else for a lifetime."
— Rachel Wolchin

My Next Step:

Keep Up with the Spirit's Leading.

How do we help one another hear and obey the Holy Spirit's leading in our lives so we can become the mature person Jesus dreamed for us to be and accomplish the mission He has invited each of us into?

[Accountability] leads to growth.

"And do not grieve the Holy Spirit of God, with whom you were sealed for the day of redemption."
– Ephesians 4:30

Introduction

The Holy Spirit is on a mission. And believe it or not, so are we!

The primary mission of the Holy Spirit in the life of a Jesus-follower is to make us like Him (2 Cor. 3:16-18). Jesus is the model we're to embrace in every way. He has lavished incredible grace on us through the Holy Spirit, who was given to us the moment we believed in Jesus.

A value within authentic community is to walk with one another as each person develops his or her serve and develops his or her gifts.

With all of God's resources at our disposal, we have the potential to work in partnership with the Holy Spirit to see the kingdom of God come alive in us and through us (2 Peter 1:3). But this supernatural transformation will remain our "potential" until we begin walking in step with the Holy Spirit to genuinely live out what we say we believe.

How we live reveals what we truly believe about God, ourselves, and our purpose in the world.

None of us live in parallel to what we believe all the time. The struggle with living perfectly is something every follower of Jesus deals with more often than we'd like to admit. Overcoming this gap between believing and behaving will be influenced by the strength of our belonging—both in Christ and in community.

"Treat a man as he is and he will remain as he is. Treat a man as he can and should be and he will become as he can and should be."
— Stephen R. Covey

When we struggle through the process of turning our faith into action, the Holy Spirit carries a deep expectation for authentic community to come together, not come apart. He doesn't want anyone to lose out on the reward Jesus has in store for those fully trusting Him with every step. The Holy Spirit can help us understand how He desires to lead us—through unbelief, brokenness, and inexperience toward faith, wholeness, and maturity—transforming us into the person God originally designed us to become.

"Each time we face our fear, we gain strength, courage, and confidence in the doing."
— Theodore Roosevelt

If we want spiritual growth to be evident in our lives, we need to move beyond embracing faith in word only. It's got to make its way into our actions if we want to share the joy of the Holy Spirit, who is working with all His energy to help us demonstrate the Jesus we believe in!

Day 1 - Become Accountable

*"[11] So Christ himself gave the apostles, the prophets, the evangelists, the pastors and teachers, [12] **to equip his people for works of service, so that the body of Christ may be built up** [13] until we all reach unity in the faith and in the knowledge of the Son of God and **become mature,** attaining to the whole measure of the fullness of Christ."*
— Ephesians 4:11-13

Building up our community is done not just through our words, but also through our actions. Our calling is to grow together in maturity as we seek to represent Jesus in our world. A healthy community desires for each person to be Christ-like, not just in the way we speak but also in they way we serve.

Read Ephesians 4:11-13.

We are commanded, "Do not bring sorrow to God's Holy Spirit by the way we live!" (Eph. 4:30) That's a strong statement. It pains the Holy Spirit when we take lightly the grace that Jesus died to give us. With this kind of grace comes great responsibility. Through the indwelling Holy Spirit, we have the capacity to represent Jesus in true form as we serve others.

Religion lulls us into being a "hearer of the Word" only, and not a "doer of the Word." Certainly, the culture of our community gives evidence to what we really believe. Ensnaring us too often, the religion trap entices us to re-create a mission that affirms our chosen lifestyle rather than accounts for our God-given ability. We need to challenge each other to ensure our lifestyle affirms the calling and the gifts we've been given as we lean into the mission of Jesus together.

We are not to be a crutch, but a catalyst in helping others engage their assignment within the mission of God.

Accountability means we must "account for our ability." Accounting for our ability sets a value that each person is an important part of the body of Christ and has an important role to play in what God is building. We should not be afraid to challenge each other to fulfill our destiny and help each other take our part seriously in bringing heaven to earth.

"You have to have confidence in your ability, and then be tough enough to follow through."
— Rosalynn Carter

1. What responsibility has God given you for which you sense a great accountability in this season of your life?

2. When does "accountability" fill you with anxiety? When does it make you feel motivated and encouraged?

Day 2 - Become Passionate

We've entered into a great mission birthed out of great passion. Jesus' love for all humanity flowed through everything He was sent to earth to accomplish. His outpouring of grace and His example of obedience forged the kingdom still flowing in the veins of His followers today. We lose passion in our heart when we lose touch with His.

*"[5] And hope does not put us to shame, because **God's love has been poured out into our hearts through the Holy Spirit**, who has been given to us." — Romans 5:5*

Read Romans 5:5.

We've been given a new heart from which we can live. The Holy Spirit, who now resides in this new heart, is passionate about raising awareness of Jesus, of His love for us and for the world. Healthy community elevates responsibility TO God out of intimacy WITH God that stirs our passion FOR God. The more we discover how God wants to accomplish His mission through us, the more we will start to feel His passion stir within us.

Jesus' heart is for us more than we can comprehend. Our belief in Him grows as we come to understand how much He believes in us, too. What an empowering and encouraging thought!

Beliefs alone don't make us a people on mission; our behavior does. He invites us to work with Him and experience the joy of seeing our world transformed. Jesus eagerly yearns to co-labor with us. It delights God to work with us in seeing His kingdom come to the earth as it is in heaven. As we gain experience in seeing God's mission fulfilled, our hearts will be filled with love *from* Him as well as *for* Him.

Beliefs don't make us a people on mission, our behavior does.

1. What does the Holy Spirit get passionate about that we should naturally get passionate about along with Him?

"Life is a gift to maximize, not an existence to endure. Live with energy and hope!" — Dennis Jeffery

2. What can you do every day to connect your heart to God's and be aware of His invitation to join Him at work around you?

Day 3 - Become Confident

When God is for us, who can be against us? Nobody! Once we begin to understand God's love for us, there's nothing that can stand in our way. God delights in inviting us into new realms of faith. We must be careful not to create judgments about ourselves that focus on our inadequacy instead of God's sufficiency.

"[37] No, in all these things ***we are more than conquerors*** *through him who loved us."*
— Romans 8:37

Read Romans 8:37.

Don't lose sight of the fact that God leads the ones He loves and equips the ones He calls. God's *vision* is always accompanied by the *provision* needed to complete what He's called us to do. You can always have confidence in God that He will never call you into anything where victory is not an option.

"I found I was more confident when I stopped trying to be someone else's definition of beautiful and started being my own."
— Remington Miller

The Holy Spirit gives us access to the character and competency we need in order to carry out every good work He has prepared for us in advance. God always provides the resources for the vision into which He calls His servants. He has gifted us, equipped us, and empowered us with the Holy Spirit, who now lives in us. It is our right to walk in boldness and take hold of everything God has waiting for us to fulfill.

God began the work in us; He will complete it. He is with us always and will never leave us nor forsake us. The Holy Spirit is not frustrated by any of our mistakes, and He experiences grief only through our lack of using what He's given us. We must believe what God says about us and what He can do in us. The result will be far more than average!

1. When and how are you tempted to disqualify yourself from doing something great with God? Where do you need a shift in thinking?

"Once we believe in ourselves, we can risk curiosity, wonder, spontaneous delight, or any experience that reveals the human spirit."
— E. E. Cummings

2. What's the difference between being "cocky" and "confident" in God's calling? How can we act boldly without being arrogant?

Day 4 - Become Holy

All Christ-followers are set apart for a greater purpose. We became holy by His grace—through our faith in Jesus' finished work on the cross—making us a new creation with a new destination. Grace not only separated us *from* sin, but separated us *for* God. Our calling is to pursue holy living because who He has made us to be must be reflected in all we do. Now we're free to work in partnership with the Holy Spirit to live a holy life—a life devoted to the mission of God for the glory of God.

*"[14] As obedient children, do not conform to the evil desires you had when you lived in ignorance. [15] **But just as he who called you is holy, so be holy in all you do;** [16] for it is written: "Be holy, because I am holy."*
— 1 Peter 1:14-16

Read 1 Peter 1:14-16.

Jesus' ways and His thoughts are higher than ours. It's our right and privilege as children of God to live from His greater paradigm. So no matter our vocation, we can play a valuable role in the mission we're on together with God. Because we're separated for His purpose, we're called to view our life, family, work, and entertainment as an opportunity to reflect our relationship with Him. We can seek elevation without discrimination, consecration without condemnation, and sanctification without segregation.

The Holy Spirit doesn't want to see anyone's journey of transformation interrupted by sin, but holiness frees us from having to fear failure, shun involvement in the lives of broken people, or avoid risks in obeying God. We didn't earn holiness through our behavior; instead, we're honored to receive it through grace. Yet, if grace is doing its work in us, it will be evidenced by what it does through us. A holy person only fears missing out on joining God to see His kingdom come to life.

"Destiny is not a matter of chance, it is a matter of choice; it is not a thing to be waited for, it is a thing to be achieved."
— William Jennings Bryan

1. What does it mean for you to be "devoted to the mission of God"?

2. What makes you afraid to take risks in obeying God, even when you know failure isn't the end of the world?

"The man who is afraid to risk failure seldom has to face success."
— John Wooden

Day 5 - Become Bold

Greater rewards require greater risks. If you want to achieve something great, you have to do something beyond the norm. As we've all heard it said: insanity is doing the same thing and expecting different results.

"[12] Therefore, since we have such a hope, ***we are very bold.****" — 2 Corinthians 3:12*

Read 2 Corinthians 3:12.

Boldness is not an option. It's a reflection. We're called to take risks to engage the adventure God has invited us into with Him. Remember, without faith it's IMPOSSIBLE to please God. We must not be afraid to thrust ourselves beyond the status quo because we only truly fail when we fail to risk obedience. Failure doesn't require us to evoke guilt, shame, fear, or condemnation but rather to engage in learning, improving, and celebrating our next step. We can know we're fully and completely loved at every stage of obedience, not just when our assignment is completed.

The pursuit of comfort, convenience, safety and security kills our passion for the mission and what the Holy Spirit is growing inside us. Bold obedience releases us from the gravity of self-absorption and missed potential.

Risk compels us to trust God in new and greater ways so we can experience Him in new and greater ways. Those in community with more experience will be taking greater risks for greater assignments while also training the next generation of sons and daughters to do the same. We risk for what lies ahead as well as for who is coming behind.

We risk in the natural, asking God to do the supernatural. We may not see or know the outcome, but we step out in joyful obedience and faith to expand God's kingdom capacity through our efforts. We must not be afraid to take hold of that for which Jesus Christ took hold of us—to accomplish His work together with Him for the glory of God!

1. Take time to pray and finish this statement: "Because of my hope in Jesus, my next step of bold obedience is to risk..."

"God's gift to you is who you are. Your gift to God is who you become." — Dallas Willard

2. Where do you need accountability for where God has given you responsibility? How can your community specifically and practically support and encourage you as you seek to accomplish it?

Group Time: Notes

[Accountability] leads to growth.

"Being filled and led by the Spirit may take you places you never planned; but the will of God will never lead you where the grace of God cannot keep you."
— Neil T. Anderson

Group Time - Session 6

Let's Start Talking

The heart of Spirit-led accountability is not calling someone out, but calling him or her up!

God wired us with the desire to make a difference and find satisfaction in accomplishing something great. That's why it's natural for us to be drawn toward people who inspire us through what they do. We often find it easy to admire the efforts of other people but don't always give ourselves the credit or celebration we deserve. We've all worked hard and have accomplished some really incredible things. Another blessing we can celebrate? Our life isn't over. We still have time for more!

1. Share one thing you are proud to have accomplished in your life, maybe one that people in your group may not know about?

2. Name one thing you would still like to accomplish someday. For whom would you jump at the chance to have coach you and help you accomplish your goal?

3. What are the biggest barriers that hinder you from attempting something you've never done before and keeps you from trying?

"[The Holy Spirit] grieves over us because He sees how much chastisement we incur, and how much communion we lose."
— C. H. Spurgeon

Week in Review

Take a few minutes to look back through your daily readings. Share with your group what you've learned and any points or questions that stood out to you this week.

Group Time - Session 6

Let's Bring It Home

You and I need strength and encouragement from the Holy Spirit and our community to help us fulfill our assignment and our potential.

Accountability simply says, "I'm with you."

One of the first miracles for a follower of Jesus to experience is the incarnation of the Holy Spirit. He brings a new beginning and a new power. The Holy Spirit is within us, constantly revealing, equipping, and calling. Though He is always for us, He graciously yet woefully endures our faulty beliefs and tepid behavior. Frankly, so do those around us who know we were made for more.

Accountability simply says, "I'm with you."

We may be overwhelmed by the fact that the Holy Spirit lives inside us and that we're part of a spiritual family on a mission bigger than we can fathom; yet feelings of insignificance are no excuse for shrugging off the heavenly blessings we possess within us. The Holy Spirit is not a petty, hypercritical weakling clamouring for attention. He is ALWAYS about elevating Jesus in our lives and in our world (John 15:26). What grieves Him should grieve us. What moves Him should move us. The more we understand His urgency, the more attentive we will be toward accomplishing the assignment Jesus has given us.

*"[26] When the Advocate comes, whom I will send to you from the Father—the **Spirit of truth** who goes out from the Father—**he will testify about me.**"*
— John 15:26

1. Why did Jesus command us not to grieve the Holy Spirit?

2. What would be different if the Holy Spirit were fully expressing Jesus' life in you and through you? How does this change how you see your potential?

"[17] For the kingdom of God is not a matter of eating and drinking, but of righteousness, peace and joy in the Holy Spirit."
— Romans 14:17

How we behave reveals what we believe.

Not living out what we believe reveals that we have a crisis of belief. Obedience will not always look the same, but it will involve the same

Group Time - Session 6

"To be yourself in a world that is constantly trying to make you something else is the greatest accomplishment."
— Ralph Waldo Emerson

level of Spirit-led behavior that elevates the life of God in us and toward others. In our own way, each of us is seeking to become an expert at hearing and obeying the Holy Spirit's leadership in our lives. Though our accomplishments are not equal, we get to celebrate each person equally, bringing a Spirit-filled joy that can be shared by all.

1. What is an assignment the Holy Spirit has been speaking to you about? What do you need in order to accomplish it?

2. Where have you lacked follow-through and need accountability for where God has given you responsibility? How can the group specifically support you as you seek to turn things around?

Accountability means giving an account for our ability. Knowing our purpose helps us lean into the Holy Spirit to grow in maturity and mission.

Elevated mission elevates devotion.

Our prayers, Bible study, and worship will climb to a whole new level when we engage our God-given assignment. Think about what a worship gathering would be like where you knew that every believer in the room was gracefully living out what he or she believed. Every heart would be full of the Spirit, with songs to sing, stories to tell, and joyful celebration that would keep us poised to live boldly and hungry for more. "On earth like it is in heaven" would be a prayer come alive!

*"[10] your kingdom come, your will be done, **on earth as it is in heaven**."*
— Matthew 6:10

Leadership is not a title; it's a way of living. Our influence is elevated by the life-giving way we serve others and by how seriously we take our responsibility to maximize our potential for making a kingdom impact.

1. Take a few minutes to publicly affirm and encourage each person around what the Holy Spirit has given them to accomplish.

Take advantage of this opportunity and begin an accountability partnership with others in your group.

2. What would an encouraging follow-up process look that helps each person follow through and accomplish their assignment?

My Response - Session 6

My Prayer Needs:

My Groups Prayer Needs:

"Confidence comes not from always being right but from not fearing to be wrong."
— Peter T. Mcintyre

My Next Step:

Give Up
My Grudges.

How do we keep our hearts open to authentic relationships and work through resentment, bitterness, and unforgiveness from hurts we have experienced in the past?

[Forgiveness] leads to freedom.

"Get rid of all bitterness, rage and anger, brawling and slander, along with every form of malice. Be kind and compassionate to one another, forgiving each other as Christ forgave you."

– Ephesians 4:31-32

Introduction

It's hard to enjoy living in the present when our hearts are still living in the past.

"We impress people with our supposed perfections but we connect with each other over our flaws."
— Donald Miller

Holding a grudge can hold us back, weigh us down, and carry serious consequences into our future. Even within a healthy community, we can step on each other's toes and hurt feelings unknowingly. In prior situations, we may have seen success in addressing the fruit of anger experienced with others, but any resentful response shows that we've yet to dig up the root from our heart. The outward circumstances may be settled, but the inward condition still needs our attention.

We must be intentional about dealing with resentment. As it grows, it gives rise to unhealthy emotions inside that soon find their way outside, able to destroy valuable relationships we've invested in so much. Those who conceal grudges shift from being loyal to being territorial while becoming critical of others and possessive of friends.

"Our bitterness goes where we go and it paralyzes our energy for mission and community."
— Dan White Jr.

A grudge will end up leading us to treat others as Satan would treat them, blaming them and their influence for the way we've chosen to act. We may believe the lie that nobody understands how hurt we are, but that's part of the devil's tactic—to use our wounds as an excuse to shut down our heart and distance ourselves from those who love us most and want to help us experience freedom.

The Holy Spirit wants to help us not only live what we believe but love like we believe.

Our calling is to love everyone, even our enemies, like Christ has loved us. It requires forgiveness from a heart that's been healed with forgiveness from Jesus. True freedom comes when we work through relational hurts and extend grace to ourselves and others involved. God's love in us will produce His love through us. We can rely on Him to help us express supernatural grace to forgive those who may have wronged us. Let's dig in!

"We are products of our past, but we don't have to be prisoners of it."
— Rick Warren

Day 1 - The Source: Hurt

"No one can make you feel inferior without your consent."
— Eleanor Roosevelt

Someone may act or respond without us in mind, yet it can still hit a nerve or bruise our ego. Though the action may not warrant it, the circumstance can hurt our pride or touch old wounds, eliciting a hostile response that can surprise the best of us.

For a follower of Jesus, a negative response most often comes from an injured heart, not an evil one. Present or past decisions, relationships, seasons, or losses can leave behind nagging injuries. Sooner or later, they'll find their way to the surface and need our attention. To understand the fruit of our pain, we have to get to the root of our pain.

"[23] Above all else, ***guard your heart, for everything you do flows from it.****"*
— Proverbs 4:23

Read Proverbs 4:23.

Our heart is the real part of us, the person we really are on the inside. The origin of every single response, whether healthy or hurtful, starts here. When our heart is wounded, what flows from it can poison our ability to love genuinely, think nobly, and see clearly. Scripture warns us to take urgent care of our heart at the first sign of contamination.

Our emotions have a purpose. They are intricately connected to our thought life and offer a sign as to the health of what's going on inside us. A bitter heart eventually will refuse any opportunity of forgiveness and reconciliation. So if you want to pursue healthy relationships from a healthy heart, don't try to hide what's inside. Let the healing begin.

It should be impossible for hurts to remain hidden in a healthy community where living from a Christ-centered identity is valued above self-centered ego, and gracious correction without condemnation is always avaiable.

1. Are there any people or situations you're involved in that make you feel afraid, upset, or angry? Would those experiences bother you if your heart were in good health? Why or why not?

2. Are there any hurts or painful experiences you need to acknowledge with God and ask Him to heal?

Day 2 - The Snare: Expectation

Getting hurt is always possible when two or more people are involved. Even the smallest offense can make a mountain out of a molehill and lead us to misrepresent our ordeal as larger than it really is. We can also foster hurt when God doesn't meet our expectations, either in His actions toward us or in the gifts He's given us. Whether with people or with God, this mindset can hinder the real outcome we're hoping to see.

Read Romans 8:28.

*"28 And we know that **in all things God works for the good** of those who love him, who have been called according to his purpose."*
— Romans 8:28

When things don't seem to go our way, there are some things we can count on: God is good, and He loves us. The person God has made us to be and the gifts He's given us are more than sufficient for the situation in which we find ourselves. We must trust that God is working out everything for our good. If it's not "good" yet, then God's not "done" yet. We will never out-sacrifice God, never out-give God, never out-forgive God, or never out-love God, so trust His heart that His best is on its way.

We may have expectations of God, but He also has expectations of us: that we respond like Jesus would toward people, even when it gets messy. It doesn't excuse any hurtful behavior by others, and it also doesn't excuse a non-Christ-like response from us. People are not to be used as a pawn for our own gratification. We must be careful when demanding our needs be met according to our own specifications. If we trust who God *is*, we will trust what God *does*. We can predict it will always turn out for our greater good and His greater purpose.

"A pharisee is hard on others and easy on himself, but a spiritual man is easy on others and hard on himself."
— A. W. Tozer

1. Is there any situation in which your hurt may be a result of unmet or unrealistic expectations you've placed on others, even God?

"People are messy; therefore, relationships will be messy. Don't be surprised by messiness."
— Tim Keller

2. In what ways can you reset expectations so you can truly appreciate the relationship again?

Day 3 - The Danger: Isolation

"Thinking in isolation and with pride ends in being an idiot."
— G. K. Chesterton

Jesus desires unity among His followers; bitterness will keep us from it.

There may be a season or situation that demands distance, but not at the expense of forgoing real healing and reconciliation. Over time, bitterness can create a huge gap between us and others around us. We can even be physically present but emotionally distant and spiritually disengaged. When we're hurting, it can be easy to isolate ourselves under the weight of emotions, but this short-term fix is not the best choice for the long-term solution we're longing for in our hearts.

*"1 An **unfriendly person pursues selfish ends** and **against all sound judgment** starts quarrels."*
— Proverbs 18:1

Read Proverbs 18:1.

The Bible is clear: Satan is like a lion seeking every opportunity to steal, kill, and destroy us (1 Peter 5:8, John 10:10). The odds quickly turn against us when we're disconnected from community. As a consequence, our imagination can run wild, our emotions can go dark, and our will can become weak—making us vulnerable to selfishness, lies, and self-absorption.

God uses those in our community to help us find healing when we're hurt and find direction when we're lost. Our friends speak gracious truth to the subtle lies we clutch. They lift us up and give us strength when we're too weak to press on. It's in these times that we need our community the most.

"Solitude is a chosen separation for refining your soul. Isolation is what you crave when you neglect the first."
— Wayne Cordeiro

Engaging the process of forgiveness doesn't mean we excuse what was done against us, but it helps us begin building a bridge of reconciliation between us and the relationships we hope to restore.

1. Do you find yourself avoiding certain people or events? Would reconnecting be a healthy step for the relationship or is it wise to keep your distance? Why?

2. What can you do to create a safe environment for someone hesitant to be his or her "true self" around you?

Day 4 - The Call: Compassion

Knowing that everyone brings his or her own personal baggage into community can help temper an unrealistic expectation of perfection.

An unhealthy perception can be our greatest deception, especially when it comes to how we treat others. Not only do our hurts affect our ability to see things clearly; the hurts others are experiencing affect how they respond as well. Inner battles are ensuing all the time in almost everyone we encounter, and we often don't take time to consider others' struggles when we're consumed with our own.

*"[32] **Be kind and compassionate to one another,** forgiving each other as in Christ God forgave you."*
— Ephesians 4:32

Read Ephesians 4:32.

Compassion is a choice we make. It begins with exchanging our perspective and emotions toward that person with those of God. It calls us to take others' hurts, wounds, and disappointment into perspective so we can more readily offer grace in the same way God has lavished it on us. When we discover that a brother or sister in Christ is trapped in a sin or unhealthy pattern, we need to take a step back and view him or her in light of God's Word—in spite of their humanity, their brokenness, and their weakness—no matter how great our struggle.

"As painful as it is to receive contempt from another, it is more debilitating by far to be filled with contempt for another."
— Arbinger Institute

Only those without sin get the option of casting the first stone; and Jesus, the only one without sin, chose death over His right to condemn others (John 3:17, Col. 2:14). Compassion demonstrates that our hearts are in alignment with God's heart. When it's not, the streaming waters of forgiveness cease to flow and our heart becomes a bitter cesspool instead of a life-giving spring.

"Love is not affectionate feeling, but a steady wish for the loved person's ultimate good as far as it can be obtained."
— C. S. Lewis

1. Why is it important for us to consider the struggles of others?

2. What would a lack of kindness and compassion for others say about your understanding of Jesus' forgiveness towards you?

Day 5 - The Cure: Forgiveness

*"[3] **So watch yourselves.** 'If your brother or sister sins against you, **rebuke them**; and if they repent, **forgive them**. [4] Even if they sin against you seven times in a day and seven times come back to you saying 'I repent,' you must forgive them.'"*
— Luke 17:3-4

Freedom requires forgiveness. It's easy to talk about, but much harder to do. Not only must we deal with the person against whom we hold a grudge but with the reality of the pain, loss, and heartache in the process. Only after we forgive will we be free of its grip.

Read Luke 17:3-4.

As Christ-followers in process, we must watch ourselves for signs that we and our community are growing in maturity, especially when it comes to forgiveness. It comes from tapping into God's supernatural power that we can access as a child of God. It's revealed in our ability to cover over a multitude of sins. But love also calls us to confront the "sinner" if we truly value the relationship. He or she deserves the opportunity to recognize it, respond to it, and resolve it with us, keeping unity alive.

"To be a Christian means to forgive the inexcusable because God has forgiven the inexcusable in you."
— C. S. Lewis

Contrary emotions may not instantly disappear the second forgiveness has been offered. We may still experience the hurt, pain, and wounds, even after forgiveness is declared. Yet the focus of forgiving is not on forgetting but on how we choose to hold onto memories after being cleansed by loving grace.

Healthy community doesn't sweep things under the carpet but learns how to engage an issue with the hope of turning a grudge into something good. Through the fruit of our actions, we can witness the Christ-like revolution being waged by the Holy Spirit and be encouraged that it's gaining ground in our hearts.

"Forgiveness is about empowering yourself, rather than empowering your past."
— T. D. Jakes

1. What causes you to shy away from confronting others when they've hurt you? How can confrontation show that you value a person?

2. How can you prepare your heart to forgive every sin against you?

Group Time: Notes

[Forgiveness] leads to freedom.

"I have always found that mercy bears richer fruits than strict justice."
— Abraham Lincoln

Group Time - Session 7

Let's Start Talking

Learning to water ski can be a humbling experience. There's nothing like being out on the open water with everyone in the boat watching you as you wobble, convulse, and hold on for dear life. Even when your skis have left your feet and the boat is dragging you head first through the water, the temptation for every beginner is to keep holding onto the rope. It sounds simple to remember but routinely causes needless pain and angst, not to mention embarrassment. As learning to release the rope is essential for novice water skiers to grasp early on, learning to release a grudge is also vital for developing healthy relationships. The earlier you recognize it, the better.

The freedom to forgive brings the freedom to live!

1. Share a time where you tried a new activity that turned out more humorous than intended.

2. Why do you think a grudge is sometimes so hard to work through, especially if you've been hurt or embarrassed?

3. In what ways is forgiveness both an event and a process?

"Everyone comes with baggage. Find someone who loves you enough to help you unpack."
— Unknown

Week in Review

Take a few minutes to look back through your daily readings. Share with your group what you've learned and any points or questions that stood out to you this week.

Group Time - Session 7

Let's Bring It Home

To experience hurt is human; to let it kill your soul is inhumane. Hurt can damage friendships over time, but holding onto hurt hurts us every time.

Forgiveness simply says, "I release you."

We must expose and do away with any feelings not rooted in love. If the Holy Spirit isn't going to entertain the same kind of feelings, then it's not the healthiest option for us either. We need to find healing for a healthier expression from the new heart God has given us.

Forgiveness simply says, "I release you."

Confession, grieving, and forgiveness are a part of the process of letting go of hurt and bitterness. Authentic community is where we have permission to process our hurt "out loud" and dump out the junk we need to get rid of without feeling belittled, judged, condemned, or rejected. It creates an environment where a hurt can be acknowledged, validated, and processed. The person feels loved while they release the unlovely things that need healing.

"[15] See to it that no one falls short of the grace of God and that no bitter root grows up to cause trouble and defile many."
— Hebrews 12:15

1. What influences your decision as to when and how you express your hurt? What makes you feel safe to share negative feelings with your community? What tends to holds you back?

2. How can we acknowledge and validate a person's pain without judging or accusing those involved unnecessarily?

"Holding a grudge doesn't make you strong; it makes you bitter. Forgiving doesn't make you weak; it sets you free."
— Dave Willis

3. What is the difference between grieving and self-pity?

4. Does forgiving someone mean condoning his or her actions?

Group Time - Session 7

Extending grace and forgiveness takes us through the process of becoming free from our past so we can fully enjoy the people God has placed in our lives today!

If we don't want to keep allowing the person who hurt us to keep hurting us, we must release our grudge. Sympathy helps console us temporarily, but forgiveness will bring release that lasts. The inner toxicity that builds up in our soul will destroy us inwardly before its effects may be noticed outwardly. For our sake and those who love us, as well as for those who will depend on our example, we must let it go and get rid of it.

When we understand the extravagant magnitude to which God has forgiven us, then and only then will we understand the compelling call to forgive others. How we impart forgiveness says more about our understanding of the grace we've received than it does about the grievance we've endured.

"Forgiveness is not an occasional act, it is a constant attitude."
— Martin Luther King Jr.

1. What may indicate that we have yet to fully forgive someone?

2. How can the gospel empower you to have compassion and genuine love toward the people you need to forgive?

"[7] During the days of Jesus' life on earth, ***he offered up prayers and petitions with fervent cries and tears to the one who could save him*** *from death, and he was heard because of his reverent submission."*
— Hebrews 5:7

Take time to offer prayers of forgiveness on behalf of those who've hurt you. Pray something like this: "I release _____ into the freedom of my forgiveness. I receive full healing through Jesus Christ to walk in the joy of my salvation."

4. What steps are important in making forgiveness permanent for your situation? How can the group come along side you and help you continue taking steps towards full healing?

"Worshiping in the midst of weakness may be among the most powerful weapons we possess on earth."
— Alicia Britt Chole

5. Take a few minutes and share what you have gained from this group and through *Authentic Community*. What's the one thing that has made the greatest impact on you personally?

My Response - Session 7

My Prayer Needs:

My Groups Prayer Needs:

My Next Step:

"Forgiveness is unlocking the door to set someone free and realizing you were the prisoner!"
— Max Lucado

Leaders
Guide.

How can you provide the best opportunity for your community to grow in their faith and experience a genuine connection with God and each another?

"And let us consider how we may spur one another on toward love and good deeds, not giving up meeting together, as some are in the habit of doing, but encouraging one another — and all the more as you see the Day approaching."

– Hebrews 10:24-25

Introduction

In church circles, we can sometime portray ourselves as people with no real problems. In reality, the opposite is true. Nobody can avoid all discouragement, distractions, and disappointment—especially when it comes to following Jesus. Scripture offers us a primary idea to consider: how can we spur on real people with real struggles—to discover real hope and find real support—in following Jesus Christ?

"Leadership is not wielding authority–it is empowering people."
— Becky Brodin

Anytime we forgo the experience of genuinely connecting our hearts with God's Word and His people, a small group can quickly lose its essential value—and influence some folks to give up on meeting. Creating space for meaningful Bible study and heart-level participation paves the way for genuine, spiritual transformation. With every opportunity, we should carefully focus our attention on the spiritual welfare of each person in the group. This is what Biblical community is truly all about.

"Needless to say, you can love people without leading them, but you cannot lead people without loving them."
— John C. Maxwell

In light of this, a small group leader's purpose lies in creating an environment in which each member can be known, loved, served, and challenged toward becoming like Jesus in every area of his or her life. Small groups offer an excellent context to facilitate this kind of involvement in one another's lives, helping each member gain the courage needed to reach his or her fullest potential in Christ Jesus.

"Encouragement is oxygen to the soul."
— George Adams

This Leaders Guide offers insights, tips, ice breakers, questions, and additional content to use as needed for helping you prepare, prior to and during the group meeting time. As a part of your weekly leadership regimen, take time to read through the *Leaders Guide* page associated with each session, review the weekly readings, look up the Bible verses, and answer the questions on your own.

"Your capacity to lead is directly related to your capacity to trust God."
— Kris Vallotton

As you prepare, ask God to open your heart to His work in your life and, through the Holy Spirit, empower you to lead others from this overflow. Remember, your main role as the group leader is to facilitate the discussion and guide the conversation. You don't need to be a Bible scholar and have all the "right answers." Just be your authentic self, feeling free to fully participate in the group and enjoy the journey toward authentic community!

"A person always doing his or her best becomes a natural leader, just by example."
— Joe Dimaggio

Creating the Environment.

Environment Prep:

1. Is it clean?

2. Does it smell nice?

3. Are all the lights on inside and outside?

4. Do we have enough chairs for everyone?

5. Are the potential distractions (animals, TV) taken care of?

6. Is the music on?

7. Am I ready to greet everyone at the door?

8. Who will gather everyone when we start the meeting?

9. Who will check the clock to make sure we start and end on time?

10. How long will everyone get to hang out after the meeting?

Sample Schedule:

6:30p	*- Meal / Snacks*
7:00p	*- Ice Breaker* *- Updates* *- Start Session*
8:00p	*- Prayer Needs* *- Ministry Time*
8:30p	*- Meeting Ends*

Touch Point: As you begin inviting others to participate in the group experience with you, ask them if they have any personal requests to be considered for the meeting (i.e., Do they have their personal copy of *Authentic Community*, a day of the week they cannot meet, dietary restrictions, physical considerations, transportation issues, work conflicts, childcare needs, etc.?). Write them down as a personal reminder and so you can appropriately communicate any needs with others in the group before the first meeting.

Meeting Prep: Think through the Group Covenant or "ground rules" that will guide your group. Consider the list below, and modify them to best represent the vision of your church's small group ministry:

1. We will accept one another where we are, as we are.
2. We will always find a way to support and encourage one another.
3. We will promise confidentiality for what we discuss with one another.
4. We will commit to growing our love for God and one another.
5. We will make this group a priority to show respect for one another.
6. We will come prepared and ready to share with one another.

If you're a part of a local church or missional community, be sure to ask your group's pastor for any direction, encouragement, or resources to help group leaders, such as how to coordinate meetings, how to deal with conflict, when to elevate sensitive issues, and whom to notify when a crisis arises in the group.

Meeting Schedule: Generally speaking, small group meetings range from 1.5 to 2.5 hours. The schedule is influenced by several key factors such as the number of people in the group, how often new people join, and the depth of care and discussion desired. Include activities for nurturing relationships such as food, ice breakers, discussion, Bible study, prayer, and post-meeting hangout time.

Leadership Tip: At every meeting, take time to personally greet every person and make him or her feel welcomed. Consider personality and potential connections with others in the group until everyone becomes socially comfortable with each other.

Session 1: Welcome to Authentic Community!

Touch Point: Prior to the group meeting, contact each person in the group by phone to remind him or her of meeting times, location, and details. Share your excitement about people's involvement and ask how you can pray for them. Write everything down so you can circle back with them about it at an appropriate time. If possible, pray with them. You'll be surprised at how encouraging it will be to them and for you.

Leader Focus: ***Help everyone connect!*** If this is your first meeting with new people in the group, don't be afraid to use name tags, and feel free to make this first meeting a little fun and a little light. Help everyone feel comfortable, stay engaged in conversation, and enjoy making a genuine connection!

Meeting Prep: Text, email, or call everyone the day before the initial meeting to remind them of the meeting details and what they may need to bring to the meeting (food, drink, funds for childcare, Bible, *Authentic Community* study guide, etc). Make sure you have the meeting environment prepared at least 30 minutes prior to arrivals.

Ice Breaker: ***"10 Things in Common"***—Draw names to divide everyone in groups of two's (or three if you have an odd number). Have each pair write down 10 things they have in common (no body parts!). The first pair to reach 10 wins! Have each pair share their list.

Before you start the Group Session in the book, have everyone share the short, two-minute version of their story.

Leadership Tip: It's essential to create a casual feel with food and drink to help set everyone at ease. Stick to the schedule, but offer plenty of time for group members to talk among themselves to ensure everyone feels more comfortable once the meeting officially begins. Start with the *Ice Breaker* to create conversation, encourage interaction, and add a little fun to the overall experience. When members shares their "short, 2-minute" version of their story, ask appropriate follow-up questions to make it more comfortable and conversational. Be sure to thank each person who shares his or her heart and is vulnerable with the group. It will set the tone for a safe environment that esteems authenticity.

Family Reminders:

1. Family makes sure nobody is embarrassed!

2. Family makes sure everyone feels good and relaxed!

3. Family keeps everything on track and on schedule!

4. Family enjoys everyone and allows everyone to be themselves!

5. Family doesn't feel the pressure to have all the answers!

6. Family isn't afraid when it gets a little emotional or a little messy!

7. Family knows when to ask, "Is it OK if we finish this discussion later?"

Do your best to start this first meeting on time, especially if everyone in the group is new. Make sure you end on time and be considerate of those with children or those with other scheduling commitments.

Session 2: Speak Up with Honesty.

Facilitating Discussion:

1. Start with simple questions that invite participation.

2. Give people time to process the question and form an answer.

3. Don't be the first to answer your own question.

4. Share your thoughts but don't talk the most.

5. Make sure to hear from those who haven't participated yet.

6. If the conversation is going well, don't feel obligated to ask every question in the book.

7. If possible, do your best to end on the final application question.

8. Take notes so you can circle back on important topics at the next meeting if needed.

9. Remember: community is built around group discussion, not personal lectures.

10. Always end with a time of prayer!

Touch Point: A day or so after your first meeting, contact each person to get insights and thoughts about how the first meeting went. Take note of their input, and pay attention to how you might adjust the meeting to be more effective. If they shared a prayer need during the group meeting, inquire about it and pray with them if appropriate.

Leader Focus: ***Help everyone feel safe to share!*** You probably already know who the extroverts and introverts are within the group. Make sure everyone gets the opportunity to be involved in the discussion. For those introverts who find it difficult to talk in a group setting, be sure to invite their input, and make sure to value and appreciate what they offer in front of the group.

Meeting Prep: Text or email everyone the day before the meeting to remind them of the meeting details and what they may need to bring to the meeting (food, drink, funds for the sitter, Bible, *Authentic Community*, etc). Share any changes you're making to the meeting based upon the group's input, and encourage everyone to be on time!

Ice Breaker: ***"Fact or Fiction?"***—Give everyone a piece of paper, and ask them to write down three things about themselves that the others in the group may not know. Make two things true and one false. Take turns allowing each person to read his or her list for the group. At the end, survey the group to find out who offered the most impressive "fiction" answer and who had the most surprising "fact."

Leadership Tip: Reinforce the *Group Covenant*, and emphasize the value of making your group a safe place for everyone to share openly and honestly. Remind everyone that what is shared in the group is to stay in the group. Acknowledge that opening up in front of others is a real challenge for some, and those who find it easy need to keep this in mind during group discussions so everyone's participation is honored.

A great conversational rule to live by: "Do your best to understand before doing your best to be understood." Being defensive means you are building a wall of division first. Ephesians 6:12 reminds us that "our struggle is not against flesh and blood," so keep your heart open.

Session 3: Make Up Quickly with Others.

Touch Point: Write a "thank you" card to each person in the group, expressing appreciation for what they shared in the prior group meeting time, and include a short prayer of encouragement. Make sure to mail it quickly so they will receive it before your next meeting.

Leader Focus: ***Help everyone deal with anger biblically!*** Hopefully, you're already experiencing transparency among the group. As each person begins to feel safe to share, emotions are guaranteed to surface. When they do, acknowledge the hurt, passion, or fear people are expressing, and validate their feelings. Those sharing their emotions for the first time will need a little grace, reassurance, and appreciation for risking vulnerability with the group.

Meeting Prep: Text or email everyone the day before the meeting to remind them of the meeting details and what they may need to bring to the meeting (food, drink, funds for the sitter, Bible, *Authentic Community*, etc). For the meeting, do your best to organize the chairs in a circle and close together. Since this sessions goes a little deeper, make sure everyone can be seen and supported during the discussion.

Ice Breaker: ***"How Do You Doo!"***—Create two teams, and take turns trying to guess as many song titles as possible in one minute. Chose one person from the team to sing first, and have the rest of the team try and guess the song. Show only the singer the song title from the cards you've prepared in advance. The catch: the singer can only sing the word "doo!" Whoever guesses the correct song becomes the singer. The team that guesses the most song titles is the winner!

Leadership Tip: At the end of this session, have everyone stand together in a circle, hold hands, and pray for the person on their left and then the person on their right. As the leader, close the group in prayer, thanking God for the freedom to share hearts, hurts, and healing together. Take time to pray specifically for anyone who stepped out in vulnerability, emphasizing the blessing of knowing hearts and affirming trust within the group. Ask God to bring healing, restoration, and peace to each life. When the prayer is over, encourage everyone to share hugs and encouragement appropriately.

Leading Through Emotion:

1. Keep direct eye contact with the person sharing.

2. Turn towards the person with undivided attention.

3. Invite him or her to share more if they desire to do so.

4. Ask follow-up questions to better understand.

5. Genuinely thank the person for sharing with the group.

6. Ask, "What do you need right now? What's the best way we can love you right now?"

7. Give him or her an appropriate level of touch to affirm your love and care for them.

8. Allow the group time to personally encourage him or her before praying and moving on.

9. Personally follow up with the person after the group meeting with caring affirmation.

10. Offer additional help like a conversation with a pastor or counselor if needed.

Session 4: Step Up and Do My Part.

Facilitating Trust:

1. Ask questions and create discussions that allow people to share their personal opinions and interests.

2. Use "ice-breakers" to help the group open up in a fun way and increase the comfort level with one another.

3. Create opportunities to play and share through a fun game or activity.

4. Serve together for a church event or community project.

5. Schedule an outing that includes a fun way to problem solve or work together as a team.

6. Create a "dinner-date" schedule to encourage one-on-one conversation before group meetings or a convenient time during the week.

7. Organize a weekend retreat or an evening out together as a group.

8. Create a weekly prayer rotation so everyone has the opportunity to spiritually connect and care for one another.

Touch Point: Follow up with each person in the group with a phone call to see how he or she is doing, and offer your perspective on the last group meeting. Affirm and celebrate the level of transparency and vulnerability demonstrated among the group. Ask them if they need anything and to confirm they will be attending the next group meeting. At this stage, being present at every meeting is crucial for maintaining true openness and building deeper trust.

Leader Focus: ***Help everyone build trust!*** A person can feel a natural tendency to pull back after becoming vulnerable with others. It's important that the group remains open and continues growing closer together, so thoughts of rejection don't have an opportunity to take hold in any relationship within the group.

Meeting Prep: Text or email everyone the day before the meeting to remind them of the meeting details and what they may need to bring to the meeting (food, drink, funds for the sitter, Bible, *Authentic Community*, etc). Take time to reflect on the prior group meeting, and refresh your memory on what was shared so you can follow up with each person at an appropriate time during the meeting. Staying in close proximity is key at this stage of authenticity, so be watchful and do your best to keep everyone connected.

Ice Breaker: ***"Twizzler Tie Up!"***—Form groups of two, and give each group five Twizzlers. The goal is to tie all five Twizzlers into a knot, but there's a catch: participants can use only one hand. The first team to tie all five Twizzlers into a knot is the winner!

Leadership Tip: Remind the group that a healthy community involves both giving and receiving. This two-way street helps everyone feel comfortable and remain connected at a heart-level. "Giving" helps us move away from self-absorption, and "receiving" helps us move away from self-isolation. All of us tend to over-compensate one way or the other when we're feeling insecure. Ask the group at some point in the discussion to identify which way they typically respond when trust feels risky, and ask what to do if the group sees him or her needing attention or shutting down.

Session 5: Build Up with My Words.

Touch Point: Craft a short, inspirational email to each person in the group. Share several examples of how he or she has contributed to the group in a positive way, and share your appreciation. End with a Bible verse and a short prayer of blessing to build and encourage their faith.

Leader Focus: ***Help everyone feel empowered!*** Engaging our God-given potential requires truth to win at every level in our lives. Speaking truth into our community is our responsibility and must be done with love, wisdom, and boldness. With so many external pressures trying to tear us down, authentic community supports our internal boldness and ability to resist temptation; it helps us "fight the good fight," strengthening us and building us up to withstand and overcome any obstacle that gets in the way.

Meeting Prep: Text or email everyone the day before the meeting to remind them of the meeting details and what they may need to bring to the meeting (food, drink, funds for the sitter, Bible, *Authentic Community*, etc). Think about each group member and what they're going through in this season of life. Take time to pray for each person according to his or her need, asking God to bless them in all they do.

Ice Breaker: ***"Word Chain!"***—The object of the game is to create a story, one word at a time. Have the group form a circle and choose one person to start. Go around the circle, and have each person add one word at a time to the story with no more than a five-second pause in between. See how long you can go and how crazy the story can get!

Leadership Tip: Give the group an opportunity to pray for each other and encourage one another on a deeper spiritual level through offering spiritual insights, impressions, and Scripture as they come to mind and heart. Scripture calls us to eagerly engage this form of encouragement motivated out of love for the building up of the Body of Christ (1 Cor. 14:1, 24-25, 31; 1 Thess. 5:19-21). Prophetic encouragement shouldn't replace, contradict, or draw attention away from God's Word, nor should it be denied. Some will be more gifted in this area than others, but present the group an opportunity to follow the Holy Spirit as He stirs up love and encouragement for others.

Empowering Scriptures:

1 Corinthians 2:9

1 Corinthians 10:31

2 Timothy 1:7

Colossians 3:2

Deuteronomy 31:6

Exodus 14:14

Galatians 6:9

Isaiah 40:31

Isaiah 41:10

Isaiah 54:17

Jeremiah 29:11

Jeremiah 32:17

Jeremiah 33:3

John 3:16

Luke 18:27

Philippians 1:6

Philippians 2:13

Philippians 4:13

Philippians 4:19

Proverbs 3:5-6

Psalm 32:8

Psalm 37:4

Romans 1:16

Romans 8:28

Romans 8:31

Romans 12:12

Session 6: Keep Up with the Spirit's Leading.

Creating Accountability:

1. INVITE - Think about someone you feel comfortable with and with whom you have a high level of trust. Leave room for them to say "no" without he or she feeling guilty or you feeling rejected by them.

2. DEFINE - Understand what accountability needs to be for you and discuss the guidelines: when to meet, how long, what questions, etc.

3. RELATE - Take time to get to know one another on a deeper level. Take a step of faith to share your story, your strengths, your struggles, and what you're striving for.

4. EXPECT - Each person must take responsibility for being truthful, transparent, and trustworthy. Come prepared to measure your own actions against your own expectations without excuse.

5. CONTEND - Fight for each other with prayerful confrontation and encouragement rooted in God's grace. Spur one another on towards victory and freedom!

Touch Point: Take a few minutes to recall a key phrase, statement, or verse that made a positive impact on the group during the prior meeting. Text or email the phrase, statement, or verse to the group with a short note. Emphasize the importance of the next group meeting, and ask them to make it a priority in prayer and attendance.

Leader Focus: ***Help everyone activate their faith!*** How we live reveals what we truly believe about God, ourselves, and our purpose in the world. A *growing* faith is a *going* faith—making the discovery, development, and deployment of spiritual gifts a priority. Our lives fall out of proportion when our level of education outweighs our level of obedience. Accountability allows those who love us to help us keep our faith in healthy perspective.

Meeting Prep: Text or email everyone the day before the meeting to remind them of the meeting details and what they may need to bring to the meeting (food, drink, funds for the sitter, Bible, *Authentic Community*, etc). Invite a few key leaders in the group to come early and pray with you over the meeting location and for each member.

Ice Breaker: *"Is It You?"*—Give each person a small piece of paper and a pen. Have everyone write down their top three personal strengths on the paper without including their name, fold it, and drop it into a basket. Randomly choose a paper from the basket, read it, and have the group try and guess who wrote it. Once the person is identified, share other strengths he or she may have that weren't written down.

Leadership Tip: Not all people understand how God has gifted them and where their strengths lie. Part of the accountability process may need to include a spiritual gifts inventory or strengths assessment to help them understand their unique gifts and potential. Consult with your small groups pastor for recommendations or for direction with utilizing an online resource. If the majority of those in your group have never taken a spiritual gifts inventory or strengths assessment, find a way to help your entire group go through an assessment before Session 6 if possible. The results can be eye-opening and provide a launching point for discussion around purpose and mission.

Session 7: Give Up My Grudges.

Touch Point: Craft a short email encouraging your group to pray about creating an accountability group or finding an accountability partner. Include the steps for "Creating Accountability" (opposite page) as a guide for them in the process; copy the "5 Steps" into an email, and send it out to the group. At the end of the email, remind everyone about this last session in *Authentic Community*. Let them know you would like to take time at the end of the session to share and celebrate what the group has gained through this study.

Leader Focus: ***Help everyone engage the process of forgiving others!*** Everyone will experience being hurt by someone at some point in their lives. In order to engage a healthy future, we need freedom from the past. Forgiving those who've hurt us is a major step toward true healing, restoration, and freedom.

Meeting Prep: Text or email everyone the day before the meeting to remind them of the meeting details and what they may need to bring (food, drink, funds for the sitter, Bible, *Authentic Community*, etc). Pray over the meeting location and each member of the group. Ask the Holy Spirit to prepare the environment as well as the heart of each person attending. Dealing with forgiveness can tap into real pain for some. Have chairs as close together as possible and tissue handy. Ask God to do a deep healing work as each person engages the process.

Ice Breaker: ***"Extreme Rock, Paper, and Scissors!"***—Divide the group into pairs. Play this game in the normal "Rock, Paper, Scissors" fashion with a fun twist. The winner continues to play the winners of other pairs, and each loser must follow the winner, chanting the winner's name. Continue until you are left with two people fighting it out, with a large crowd of supporters watching!

Leadership Tip: At the end of the group meeting, gather suggestions of other small groups or individuals who would benefit from going through *Authentic Community*. Ask the group members to join you in reaching out to those mentioned, sharing your experiences through this study and encouraging them in starting a new group. It's a simple way to continue fostering a culture of authenticity within your church.

Practicing Forgiveness:

1. Identify the wound.
2. Identify the offense.
3. Identify the offender.
4. Release the offense.
5. Release the offender.
6. Receive His healing.

Jesus' Forgiveness:

"Do not judge, and you will not be judged. Do not condemn, and you will not be condemned. Forgive, and you will be forgiven."
— Luke 6:37

Jesus said, "Father, forgive them, for they do not know what they are doing."
— Luke 23:34

"When they hurled their insults at him, he did not retaliate; when he suffered, he made no threats. Instead, he entrusted himself to him who judges justly."
— 1 Peter 2:23

"Bear with each other and forgive one another if any of you has a grievance against someone. Forgive as the Lord forgave you."
— Colossians 3:13

Leader Notes:

Leader Notes:

For additional resources, go to:
http://jasonlohse.com.

For invoice billing requests on bulk orders, contact:
info@jasonlohse.com.

Made in the USA
Columbia, SC
27 February 2018